How to design
and make your own

QUILTS

How to design and make your own

QUILTS

KATHARINE ■ GUERRIER

MALLARD
PRESS

MALLARD PRESS

An imprint of BDD Promotional
Book Company, Inc.,
666 Fifth Avenue,
New York, N.Y. 10103

Mallard Press and its accompanying logo
are trademarks of
BDD Promotional Book Company, Inc.

First Published in the United States of America in
1991 by the Mallard Press

ISBN 1-7924-5534-7

This book was designed and produced by
Quintet Publishing Limited
6 Blundell Street
London N7 9BH

Creative Director: Terry Jeavons
Art Director: Ian Hunt
Designer: Annie Moss
Editor: Caroline Beattie
Illustrators: Katharine Guerrier & Danny McBride

Typeset in Great Britain by
Central Southern Typesetters, Eastbourne
Manufactured in Hong Kong by
Regent Publishing Services Limited
Printed in Hong Kong by
Leefung-Asco Printers Limited.

Picture Credits
~ ~

*The Author and the Publishers would like to thank the following
for lending their work for reproduction in this book:*

Jacket front: made by Katharine Guerrier, photo by Neil Woolford;

Back Jacket: made by Katharine Guerrier, photo by John Coles;

10, 11, 12: photo Ian Howes;

14: top left: made by Katharine Guerrer, photo by Ian Howes;

top right: Reproduced by permission of the American Museum in Britain, Bath;

bottom left: made by Katharine Guerrier, photo by Ian Howes;

bottom right: photo by Ian Howes;

24: made by Carole Proctor, photo by Ian Howes;

26: made by Jenny Hall, photo by Ian Howes;

27: made by Katharine Guerrier, photo by Ian Howes;

28: photo by Ian Howes;

30: made by Moira Robertson, photo by John Coles;

*33 top: Reproduced by permission of the American Museum in Britain, Bath,
photo by Derek Palmer; bottom: made by Katharine Guerrier, photo by Ian Howes;*

34: made by Katharine Guerrier, photo by Ian Howes;

35: made by Moira Robertson, photo by John Coles;

36 top: Reproduced by permission of the American Museum in Britain, Bath;

bottom: made by Katharine Guerrier, photo by Ian Howes;

37: Reproduced by permission of the American Museum in Britain, Bath;

40: Reproduced by permission of the American Museum in Britain, Bath;

41: made by Katharine Guerrier, photo by Ian Howes;

43 left: made by Katharine Guerrier, photo by Ian Howes;

right: made by Nancy S. Breland;

44: Reproduced by permission of the American Museum in Britain, Bath;

45: made by Katharine Guerrier, photo by Neil Woolford;

47: made by Katharine Guerrier, photo by Ian Howes;

49, 50, 52: made by Katharine Guerrier, photo by John Coles;

53: made by Alison Kirkby, photo by John Coles;

57: Reproduced by permission of the American Museum in Britain, Bath;

58 left: made by Katharine Guerrier, photo by Ian Howes;

58 right, 59: Reproduced by permission of the American Museum in Britain, Bath;

61: made by Jean Gage, photo by Charles Gage;

62: made by Katharine Guerrier, photo by Viewfinders, Sheffield;

63 top: made by Adele Outtridge, photo by Ian Tudor;

bottom: made by Katharine Guerrier, photo by Ian Howes;

64, 65: made by Katharine Guerrier, photo by Neil Woolford;

68, 69: made by Katharine Guerrier, photo by Ian Howes;

71: made by Katharine Guerrier, photo by Neil Woolford;

72, 74: made by Carole Proctor, photo by Neil Woolford;

75: made by Katharine Guerrier, photo by John Coles;

76: made by Katharine Guerrier, photo by Viewfinders, Sheffield;

77, 78: made by Katharine Guerrier, photo by Ian Howes.

Contents

INTRODUCTION
~

*A*t face value a patchwork quilt is a colourful bedspread or wall hanging. A closer investigation of this fascinating craft reveals a multi-faceted subject which spans history, the aesthetics of design and colour combined with practical sewing skills.

The origins of patchwork, which together with appliqué and quilting make up the craft of quiltmaking, are lost in history. Examples of patchwork have been found in the Egyptian tombs and in archeological remains on the old silk road between China and India, and it is conjectured that Joseph's coat of many colours in the Old Testament may have been patchwork. Certainly, patchwork items are known to have been brought back from the East by the Crusaders, but it was not until the 17th and 18th centuries, when the East India Trading Company started to import fine printed cotton into Britain, that patchwork became a fashionable pastime for leisured middle- and upper-class ladies. The popularity of these imported Indian

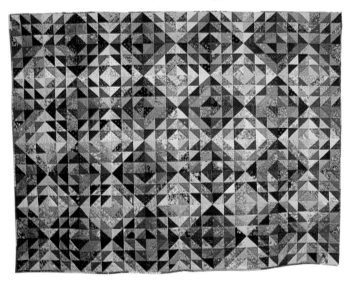

chintzes posed a threat to the British textile manufacturers who could not yet match the quality in colour and printing; they pressed for trade restrictions, making the fabrics scarce and expensive. Every tiny scrap was hoarded to be used in patchwork and appliqué, to make a little go a long way. The resulting quilts which survived from this period are the fine chintz appliqué and patchwork mosaic quilts, the earliest of which dates from 1708 and can still be seen at Levens Hall in Cumbria, Great Britain.

Alongside these fine quilts, made in scarce and expensive materials by the middle and the upper classes, was another type of patchwork made strictly for utilitarian purposes by the working classes. The materials used in these quilts was often homespun or the less expensive cotton fabrics manufactured and printed in Britain. Simple shapes such as triangles, squares and diamonds were pieced together with a running stitch, more economical in time than the laborious 'paper piecing' or 'English' method which allowed for more intricate shapes.

The settlement of North America was the next significant factor in the development of the patchwork quilt. Contrary to expectations, the first colonists found a hostile environment awaiting them. Basic supplies were short and to repair and recycle was the order of the day. Trade restrictions, which forced the Colonists to buy fabrics from Britain, made them not just expensive but virtually unobtainable, so scraps of fabric were hoarded and used in the first American patchwork quilts. These were utilitarian and with little planned design. As life became more settled, the quilt makers began to develop the traditions and designs which were to become uniquely American.

Limited space in many homes meant that it made sense to construct a quilt in units which could be easily worked on the lap. Designs for these units, or 'blocks', were evolved first by folding paper. An additional advantage to this type of quilt construction was that the blocks could be stacked away ready for assembly when enough had been completed.

Many of the activities necessary for survival in the New World required the involvement of the whole community. Barn raising, harvesting and corn husking were cooperative efforts and a quilting bee, or party, was also a cooperative activity. Finished quilt tops pieced through the winter were set up with the filler and backing on the quilting frame and as many women as could fit around the edge stitched the three layers of the quilt together, often in just one day. Others helped by threading needles or preparing food for the large

social gathering that followed – which was an important social occasion and an event to look forward to for those women isolated by rough roads and bad weather through the winter.

By the time of her marriage, a young woman was expected to have pieced up to twelve quilt tops, and often a thirteenth was made by her friends as a gift on her wedding day. This was the only quilt on which hearts and lovers' knots could be stitched; it was considered unlucky to use such motifs on any other quilt. Designs developed and evolved, many of the blocks being given names which were related to the environment, historical events or famous personalities. 'Rocky Road to Kansas', 'Sherman's March' and 'Martha Washington's Star' were all well-known block designs.

Alongside the everyday quilts made for constant use, beautiful quilts with more intricate shapes and difficult designs were produced. When completed these were only used on special occasions or for favoured guests, and this is why many of the surviving quilts are so elaborate: the plainer, everyday ones just wore out. Notable among the quilt designs are those of the Amish community. Boldly coloured, handsomely quilted and graphically geometric, they attract a well-deserved following in the quilt world.

During the 19th century, due to increased affluence, fashions in quilt-making changed. Elaborate appliqué and crazy quilts became popular, the latter being made in rich fabrics like silk and satin embellished with embroidery and symbolic motifs such as horse shoes, flags and eagles.

In the early years of the 20th century, quilt-making suffered a decline; the easy accessibility of machine-made bedding and employment outside the home meant that there

was no longer the necessity or the time for women to make quilts. Then, after a long period when quilts were considered old-fashioned and often consigned to the attic or garage, there was a revival of interest starting in the late '60s and the '70s.

This renewed interest has inspired many people to experiment with quilt-making on all levels, from the simplest traditional designs to the most elaborate investigation with colour and pattern, elevating the status of quilt-making from folk art to fine art. The reasons for making patchwork quilts today may be very different from those which motivated the early quilt makers, but patchwork still remains a most accessible form of creativity, based on attainable principles of design, constructed with the most elementary materials and producing something which not only has terrific visual and tactile appeal but serves the most essential of purposes.

Chapter One

Materials & Equipment

~

"*For the greater number of women . . . the nostalgic value of the craft (patchwork), the fact that it puts them in spiritual contact with women before them, remains vitally important.*"

Michael James. *Quilt Art*, Catalogue to the 1986 Quilt Art UK. Touring Exhibition

Fabrics and Fillings for Patchwork

The renewal of interest in patchwork over the last decade has led to a much greater availability of the pure cotton fabrics, which are ideally suited to it. Look through the small ads of any of the patchwork and sewing magazines and you will find mail order firms offering huge selections of printed and plain-coloured fabrics. By sending for their sample packs you will discover the almost unlimited choice available to the patch-worker. Investigate other sources such as remnant boxes in department stores, market-stalls and dressmaking off-cuts. Polycotton sheeting, poplin, fine needle-cord and cotton lawn can all be used in patchwork as can the lighter weights of furnishing fabric. Keep your eyes open for suitable fabrics and start a collection – ¼ to ½ yd or metre pieces are often all you need for your first projects. Most of the fabrics available specifically for patch-work are either plain or small prints, but larger prints can often be used to good effect so do not discount them. Silks, vel-vets and taffetas can give patchwork quilts a rich surface texture, but as they are more difficult to handle it may be advis-able to save these for a later project when you have gained some experience. Re-member that any fabric with a one-way pile or nap, such as needlecord, corduroy or velvet, will appear to change colour if the direction of a pile is changed.

Think about how your quilt is to be cleaned or laundered – cotton is by far the most practical fabric for a quilt that will be used as a bedcover. Save the more exotic fabrics for decorative projects such as a wall-hanging or door curtain.

Try to use similar weights of fabric to-gether; putting a fine cotton lawn next to corduroy would only lead to puckering and uneven wear. However, lighter fabrics can be made firmer by using a dress-maker's interfacing on the back.

Stretch or knit fabrics are not suitable for patchwork; a fabric that may go out of shape during the making of a quilt could distort the fit and ruin your design.

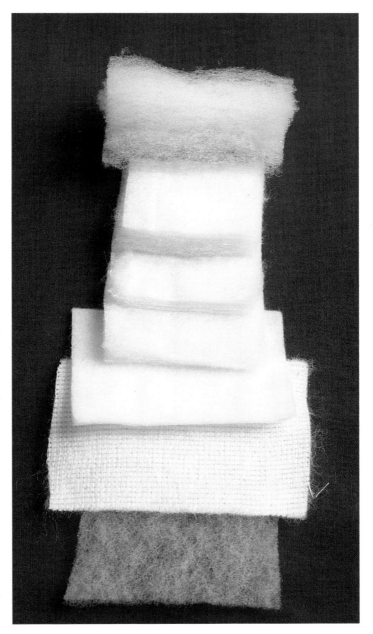

Always wash fabrics before using them to shrink and test for dye fastness. If dye leaks out, continue to rinse until the water runs clear. If using old garments, cut away and discard any worn or faded parts.

WADDING OR BATTING

Choice of a quilt filler (the warm interlin-ing between top and backing) can be con-fusing because there are different types. How you plan to finish the quilt and the purpose for which it is made will affect this choice.

The most economical filler is the poly-ester wadding (batting), which is available in a variety of weights. For quilting by hand or machine the 2-oz weight is the most practical. Thin enough to stitch through easily, while providing a warm, light interlining for the quilt, it is washable and will not shrink or disintegrate in use even with minimal quilting. The heavier weights (3–6 oz) are suitable for tied quilts and will give a puffy, scrunchy appearance to comforters. Another advantage to the polyester waddings is that they are avail-able in large pieces, big enough for king and queen-size quilts, so there is no need to join pieces for these larger sizes. For smaller projects, wadding (batting) is also available on rolls of different widths. One disadvantage to polyester is that it will blunt scissor-blades and machine needles quite quickly, but this is far outweighed by the advantages.

Needlepunched polyester wadding (batting) is more compact and solid, having been through a flattening process under hundreds of needles, which reduces the thickness while maintaining the weight. This gives a flatter effect suitable for wall-hung quilts.

A cotton filler is the traditional material for quilts – originally teased and carded flat by the quilt-maker, it is now available, prepared for you, by the yard and will give a flatter and more 'antique' look to your quilt, but it is more difficult to work with. It comes off the roll folded with a papery outer skin, and has to be opened out carefully exposing the loose fibres. As cotton will not hang together like polyester it must be closely quilted to keep it in position. The manufacturers recommend that quilts with cotton fillers are dry cleaned; they cannot be pre-shrunk as the filler would disintegrate.

'Cotton Classic' has overcome many of the disadvantages whilst retaining the quality of pure cotton wadding (batting). It is 80 per cent cotton and 20 per cent polyester and has bonded surfaces making it easier to handle. It is also possible to pre-shrink it: to do this put the wadding (batting) into a cotton bag (eg a pillowcase), immerse in hot water and then give it a short spin in the washing machine. Now remove the wadding from the bag, shake it out gently and hang it in a warm place to dry out. Some people like the slightly 'antique' look which occurs when the finished item is washed and the wadding shrinks slightly, puckering the surface fabric.

Pure silk wadding (batting) is now available on the roll, and quilted with silk thread will give your quilt a luxury feel. However, it is expensive and is probably best reserved for small projects or garments.

Terylene or cotton domette (manufactured as warm curtain interlining) is a good filler for wall-hangings and door curtains. It gives a flat surface and a good weight.

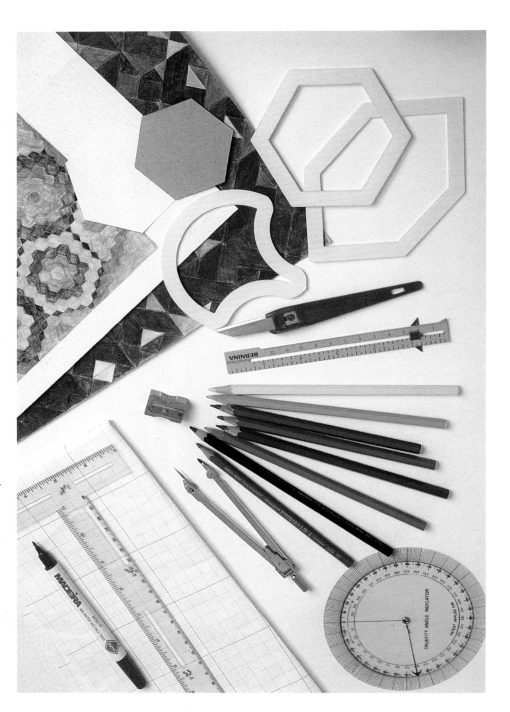

ABOVE Useful design tools for patchwork.

~

Watch the manufacturers' advertisements as new products appear regularly, and if in doubt about your choice of quilt filler send to the supplier for samples. Although unseen, the inside layer of the quilt is as important as the two outer layers.

BACKING

Observe people looking at an exhibition of quilts and you will see many of them pick up the corners of the quilt and look at the back. Are they examining the quality of the stitching, or trying to gain an insight into the maker by seeing what has been chosen for the backing? They would be surprised to find in the American Museum, England, a unique double-sided quilt made by two sisters, each side as intricately pieced as the other, but for the underside of a quilt a whole piece of fabric is more usual.

If you are planning to quilt by hand, choose a fairly soft cotton backing so that your needle will go through the three layers easily. Match the weight of the backing to the fabrics used in the quilt top. Sheeting is available in widths up to 108 in (275 cm) but is not recommended for hand-quilting as the weave is too close-textured, making it difficult to stitch through, but it would be suitable for a machine-quilted piece. If you need to join lengths of fabric to make up the size – which should be approximately 4 in (10 cm) larger all round than the quilt size – you will need to cut off the selvedge first because it has a tendency to draw in the edge slightly and cause puckering. Press the seams open.

Remember that a patterned backing fabric will disguise the quilting stitches whereas a plain coloured one will show them off.

Equipment

Essential equipment for patchwork is the same as for dressmaking with one or two additions.

SCISSORS

Keep one pair of sharp scissors only for cutting out fabric, and another pair especially for paper since paper blunts scissors fairly quickly. A pair of fine embroidery scissors is useful for snipping threads and trimming seam allowances.

PINS

The glass-headed variety are easier to see, and they are longer and finer. Keep pins in a pin-cushion rather than a tin as this will make them easier to retrieve when you drop them.

Wedding dress pins are also long and fine, and are suitable for delicate fabrics.

NEEDLES

A variety of sizes is useful. For hand-sewing patches together use sharps number 8 or 9, which are fine and long enough to take three or four stitches at a time. For quilting, short fine needles are best, betweens number 8 or 9 (the higher the number the smaller the needle).

THREAD

You will need a selection of threads for hand and machine sewing. You will find that you add to the colours as you progress, and build up a collection. When sewing patchwork, try to match the thread to the fabric as far as possible. If in doubt, always use a darker thread in preference to a lighter one. Likewise, when sewing a dark patch to a light one use a thread that matches the dark patch.

Quilting thread is thicker than machine thread, and it is better for hand-quilting and sewing.

A THIMBLE

A thimble that fits may be hard to find but is well worth looking for. It will protect your finger and enable you to sew for much longer. Although it may seem uncomfortable to use at first, it is worth persevering if you intend to do a lot of hand-stitching. If you cannot get on with a metal one try the leather type.

WAX

This will prevent knotting and strengthen thread when hand-stitching.

TAPE-MEASURE

An essential item in any workbox, most now have both imperial and metric measurements.

UNPICKER, SEAM RIPPER

More efficient than scissors for unpicking small stitches.

IRON

Patches and seams must be well pressed so either a good steam iron, or a dry iron and mist sprayer, is essential.

SEWING-MACHINE

This will speed up the process of construction for the American method, but all patchwork can be stitched by hand.

FABRIC MARKER

Choose one with which you can get a fine line on the fabric. The fading type of felt-tip marker is a good choice. The line will fade after 24 hours.

SEAM-ALLOWANCE MEASURE

Useful for small measurements.

The seam allowance used in patchwork is ¼ in (6 mm) so a quilter's quarter – a ruler with ¼ in (6 mm) sides all round – is a useful tool both for checking these and making templates.

Cutting out *must* be accurate and takes longer than the actual construction in patchwork, so you may want to invest in a rotary cutter and self-healing board, which will speed up the process. A certain amount of practice will be needed to acquire the skill to use the cutter.

Equipment for Designing

CARTRIDGE PAPER

For papers used in the English method (Chapter 2), but used envelopes or paper of a similar weight will do just as well.

SQUARED GRAPH PAPER

For designing and making templates.

ISOMETRIC GRAPH PAPER

Marked out in triangles, this provides an accurate way of making templates for hexagons and diamonds in any size. It is also useful for planning a quilt which uses these shapes.

A BASIC GEOMETRY SET

A set containing compasses, a protractor and a set square.

COLOURED PENCILS AND FELT TIP PENS

It is always useful to try out different colour combinations at the planning and designing stage.

AN ACCURATE RULER

For drawing and measuring templates.

TEMPLATES

A basic set in metal or plastic is a useful starting point, but you will soon want to make your own so that you have more freedom in design. They can be made from good-quality card using a metal ruler and a craft knife or scalpel. It is important to cut them accurately.

MAKING TEMPLATES FOR ENGLISH PATCHWORK

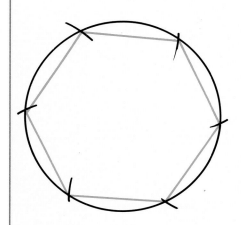

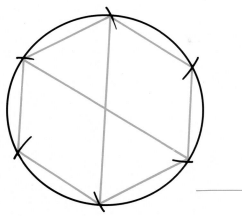

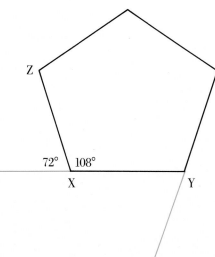

HOW TO DRAW A HEXAGON Set compass to the desired length of hexagon's sides and draw a circle. Using the same radius, place the compass point anywhere on the circle and draw an arc crossing the circle's circumference. Now place the compass point on the crossing point and draw another arc. Continue around the circle until you have 6 crosses. Join these with straight lines to form a hexagon.

DIAMOND Draw a hexagon then connect opposite points to form two diamonds and two equilateral triangles.

PENTAGON Draw a line xy the desired length of the sides. From point x, mark a point z at 108° to the line xy using a protractor. Mark off the correct length on the line xz. Repeat until you have drawn the 5 sides.

Making Templates

The sewing method will determine the type of template you need. For the English method of patchwork, where the pieces of fabric are tacked (basted) over papers and whip-stitched together, the basic template for cutting out the paper pieces should be the size of the finished patch. If a metal or plastic template in the correct size and shape is available then buy one as they are more durable. If you cannot buy the one you need it is possible to make one with a basic geometry set. Any shape or combination of shapes which fit together without leaving a gap (tesselate) can be used in English patchwork. The need for accuracy cannot be stressed enough when making templates. Use a sharp hard pencil (2H) to draw with and cut the template from stiff (though not thick) card using a craft knife and metal ruler.

WINDOW TEMPLATES

These enable you to frame a specific part of the fabric you are using in order to centre a motif. Draw the size and shape of the desired patch on to card, then draw a second outline ¼ in (6 mm) bigger all round. Cut out the centre shape and around the outside line. You can mark the cutting line for the patch around the outside of the template and the stitching line around the inside of the template.

TEMPLATES FOR AMERICAN PATCHWORK

In order to plan a repeat block quilt (a design in which a design unit, or block, is repeated throughout the quilt) you need to be able to draw and cut templates. This will give you the freedom to adapt traditional block designs, and enable you to change the size of a block, add a border or combine features together from more than one quilt.

WINDOW TEMPLATES

patch size

cutting line

Centering a motif using a window template.

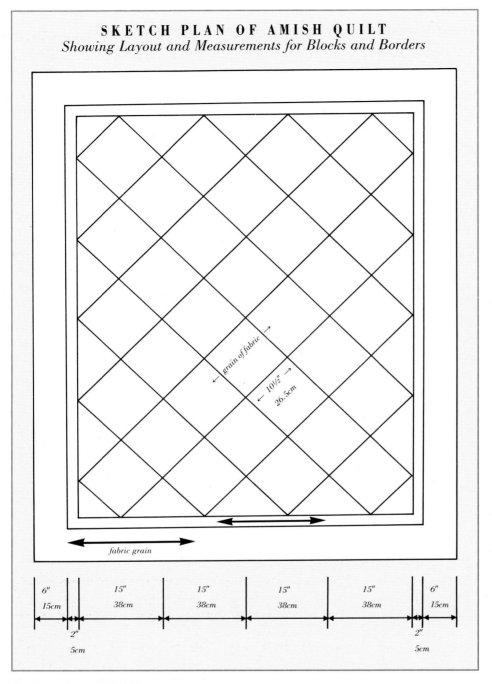

SKETCH PLAN OF AMISH QUILT
Showing Layout and Measurements for Blocks and Borders

grain of fabric

10½"
26.5cm

fabric grain

6"	15"	15"	15"	15"	6"
15cm	38cm	38cm	38cm	38cm	15cm

2"
5cm

2"
5cm

First decide on the finished size of the quilt, which will affect the size of the blocks you will use. Now draw a sketch plan of the quilt and make a note of the measurements required in each part of it, eg, blocks and borders, in order to fit the design to the final size of the quilt. The technique of drafting patterns and cutting templates is demonstrated here using the Churn Dash block (Chapter 4), and it can be used for any geometric block. The quilt in question is 70 in (175 cm) × 85 in

(212 cm). To fit the design to this size the blocks must be 15 in (38 cm) from point to point diagonally, the narrow border must be 2 in (5 cm) wide and the broad outer border 6 in (12.5 cm). Any of these measurements could be altered to adjust the size of the quilt. When you have decided on the relative sizes of each part, work out the block size, which in this case would be a 10½ in (26.5 cm) square to give a diagonal measurement of 15 in (38 cm).

Next, identify the grid within the patchwork block. In this case it is 3 × 3, known as a nine-patch, so the block must be equally divided into nine 3½ in (9 cm) squares. Draw the block pattern full size onto a piece of squared graph paper and identify the different shapes you will need to make up the pattern. In this case three: a triangle, a square and a rectangle. Cut one of each accurately from your full-size drawing, using either paper scissors or a craft knife, and stick these pieces onto thin card right sides up with stick glue. For hand-stitched American patchwork cut the card carefully, flush with the edges of the graph paper.

For machine stitched American patchwork ¼ in (6 mm) seam allowances must be added before cutting out the templates. Using a quilter's quarter add ¼ in (6 mm) seam allowance to all sides of each shape. You will find that you can butt the quilter's quarter against the shape you have mounted on the base card and draw a fine line around it, giving the correct seam allowance. Cut around this exactly and label each piece with the name and size of the block (Churn Dash 10½ in (26.5 cm) block). Keep them together in an envelope with a small sketch of the block on squared paper as a reference.

Calculating Fabric for Patchwork

To calculate the quantity of fabric you will need for a specific project count how many times each template will be used for any one fabric, adding seam allowances if these are not already part of the templates. Divide the number of times the template width fits across the fabric width into the number of patches needed in that fabric and multiply that by the length of the template. Round this up to the nearest ¼ yd (20 cm). It may help to draw a sketch plan of the fabric noting measurements and drawing the shapes onto it. See the sample sketch plan of the plain fabric needed for the Pinwheel cot quilt. By buying a little extra fabric each time you start a new project you will soon build up a collection to draw from for future scrap quilts.

MAKING TEMPLATES FOR AMERICAN PATCHWORK

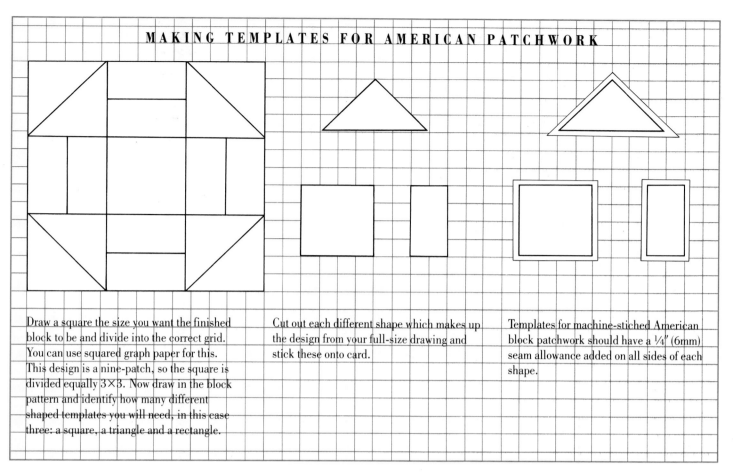

Draw a square the size you want the finished block to be and divide into the correct grid. You can use squared graph paper for this. This design is a nine-patch, so the square is divided equally 3×3. Now draw in the block pattern and identify how many different shaped templates you will need, in this case three: a square, a triangle and a rectangle.

Cut out each different shape which makes up the design from your full-size drawing and stick these onto card.

Templates for machine-stiched American block patchwork should have a ¼" (6mm) seam allowance added on all sides of each shape.

ESTIMATING FABRIC
Sketch Plan of Plain Fabric Needed for Pin-Wheel Cot Quilt

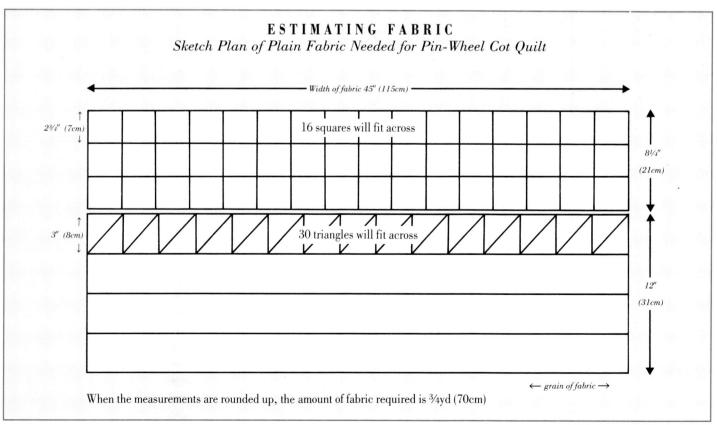

When the measurements are rounded up, the amount of fabric required is ¾yd (70cm)

ENGLISH PATCHWORK

← grain of fabric →

PREPARING THE PATCHES Cut paper shape using template and pin to the wrong side of the fabric. Cut the fabric patch ¼"–⅜" (6mm–9.5mm) bigger than the paper all round.

Fold the fabric over the paper ensuring that the edge of the paper is right into the fold and tack (baste) through all layers. At the corners fold the fabric over and secure with a stitch. Finish with one or two backstitches.

JOINING THE PATCHES Place patches right sides together and oversew neatly. Try not to catch the paper in the stitching. Begin either with a knot concealed in the seam allowance or 2–3 backstitches and fasten off firmly with backstitches.

centre hexagon

MAKING THE ROSETTES: join the centre patch to one of the side patches. Continuing with the same thread connect third patch to second side of second patch. With a new thread, join the second side of the centre patch to the third patch, and continue with the same thread to attach third side of third patch to fourth patch. Keep adding hexagons until rosette is complete.

Preparing and Sewing Patches – English Method

Using a template and hard pencil (2H), draw and cut out the shape required from firm paper. Cut each of the papers one at a time; cutting several layers together will distort the shape and lead to problems when fitting patches together. That could throw out your whole quilt. Pin the paper to the wrong side of your fabric and cut out the patch approximately ¼ in (6 mm) larger than the paper all round. The grain of the fabric, that is, the way the woven threads lie, should run the same way throughout a piece of patchwork, so bear this in mind when positioning the paper onto the fabric. If you want to use the fabric in a particular way, eg, stripes going around in a circle, then disregard this rule. Fold the seam allowance over the paper and tack (baste) firmly; finish stitching with one or two back stitches. Use a contrasting thread for this, which makes the later removal of tacking (basting) and papers easier.

Press the patches to form a sharp crease and place them right sides together, lining up the edges to be stitched. Oversew the patches together using matching thread where possible, a darker one in preference to a lighter one if in doubt, and a dark thread when sewing a light patch to a dark one. Begin stitching either with a knot concealed in the seam allowance or with two or three small back stitches, and finish firmly with back stitches. Avoid catching the paper with your stitching. When patches are joined to their neighbours on all sides, the papers can be removed and re-used several times.

When making up hexagon rosettes, begin by attaching the centre hexagon to one of the side hexagons. Take a third hexagon and continue stitching with the same thread round the corner to join the second and third hexagons. With a new piece of thread attach the second side of the centre hexagon to the third patch and continue round the corner to attach the fourth hexagon. Continue in this way until the rosette is complete. Make sure that your stitching goes right into each corner so that there are no gaps.

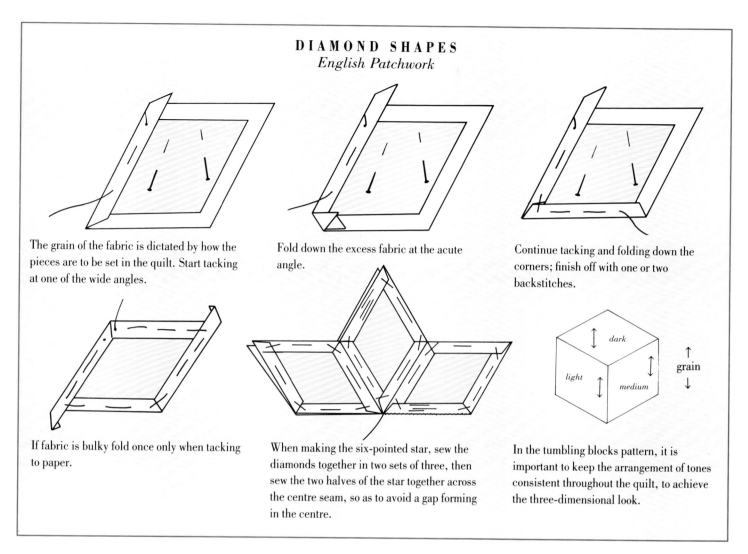

DIAMOND SHAPES
English Patchwork

The grain of the fabric is dictated by how the pieces are to be set in the quilt. Start tacking at one of the wide angles.

Fold down the excess fabric at the acute angle.

Continue tacking and folding down the corners; finish off with one or two backstitches.

If fabric is bulky fold once only when tacking to paper.

When making the six-pointed star, sew the diamonds together in two sets of three, then sew the two halves of the star together across the centre seam, so as to avoid a gap forming in the centre.

In the tumbling blocks pattern, it is important to keep the arrangement of tones consistent throughout the quilt, to achieve the three-dimensional look.

DIAMONDS – ENGLISH METHOD

The acute angles on a diamond shape make it a little more difficult to tack (baste) fabric to paper. Pin the paper to the wrong side of the fabric and cut out the patch, allowing ¼ in (6 mm) seam allowance as for hexagons. Begin tacking at one of the oblique (wide) angles. When you reach the acute angle of the diamond, fold the fabric over twice, being careful not to fold the paper into the first fold. The excess fabric in the seam allowance will now be on the wrong side of the patch making it easier to stitch patches together. If you are using bulky fabric, fold the fabric once, leaving a tab at the acute angle. This must be manoeuvred to the back when stitching the patches together.

When making a six-pointed star with diamonds, stitch the diamonds together in two sets of three, then place the two halves of the star together and sew the centre seam right across, thus avoiding having a gap in the centre where all the points meet.

The tumbling blocks pattern, made by sewing three diamonds together, is quite straightforward. Just ensure that the stitching goes right into the corners, so that no gaps occur which would cause a weakness in the patchwork.

If you are making a panel of English patchwork to appliqué onto a background (a Dresden Plate motif for example), press the patchwork with a steam iron or under a damp cloth when you have finished assembling it, before carefully removing the papers. This creates a sharp crease around the outer edge. Tack (baste) down the turnings around the outer edge before positioning the work onto the background, then pin and tack down the motif,

smoothing it flat over the background, and stitch neatly by hand or machine. Lastly, remove all tacking stitches.

FINISHING ENGLISH PATCHWORK

More often than not the shapes used in English patchwork do not give the quilt top straight edges, but there are various ways of solving this problem.

For the first method: when the patchwork is finished, press the edges before carefully removing the papers. Then draw a straight line along the sides of the patchwork where the border or binding is to be attached. Now cut through the patchwork along this line. This makes it possible to attach a straight or mitred border to the patchwork as described in 'Borders' (see below).

Another method is to appliqué the edges of the patchwork to a straight border. To

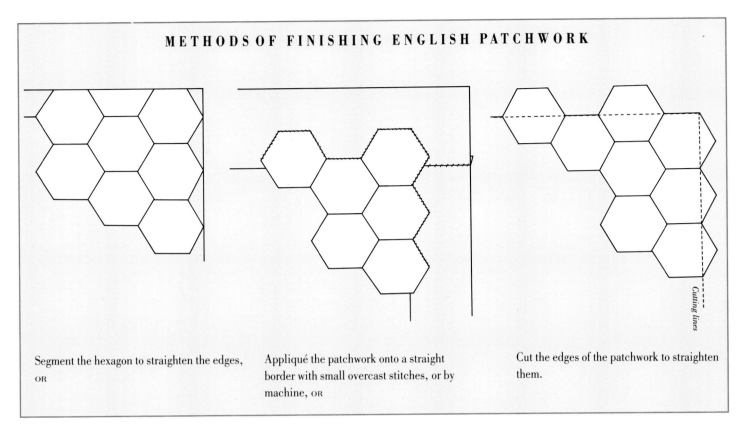

METHODS OF FINISHING ENGLISH PATCHWORK

Segment the hexagon to straighten the edges, OR

Appliqué the patchwork onto a straight border with small overcast stitches, or by machine, OR

Cut the edges of the patchwork to straighten them.

Cutting lines

do this cut two border strips for the shorter sides first. Make them wide enough to form a border on the wrong side of the patchwork as well, and long enough at each end to accommodate the borders for the longer sides which are added later. Turn under the long edge of the side which is to go under the patchwork, by pressing ¼ in (6 mm) of fabric to the wrong side, and then pin and stitch the patchwork to the border by hand or machine. Now cut the borders for the longer sides to the same width, and long enough to reach under the border on the shorter sides. Pin and stitch the patchwork onto the long borders, then slip hem the short borders onto the long borders (refer to the diagram).

Or you can segment the hexagon and cut papers to fit the gaps round the sides. Cover the papers as you would for complete hexagons and fit and stitch these into the gaps thus straightening the sides of the patchwork. When finished like this, the edges of the patchwork are folded under. Press firmly to fix the creases before removing the papers. Now stitch the straight sides to border strips as for the appliqué method.

Preparing and Sewing Patches – American Method

HAND STITCHED

When making up blocks in American patchwork the grain of the fabric should run parallel with the straight sides of the block. Mark a straight line on each template to indicate how you will position it on the fabric. Place the template on the wrong side of your fabric, remembering to turn over any asymmetrical template, for example, a rhomboid, so as not to cut a mirror image patch. Draw around each template with a fabric marker leaving enough space between them to add seam allowances when cutting out. Since the line you have marked is the stitching line, cut out each shape adding a ¼ in (6 mm) all around the marked line. You can either draw the cutting line onto the fabric or measure by eye. When you have cut out all the patches in one block, place them together on a flat surface in the correct positions.

ORDER OF PIECING

The two basic rules are to start with the smaller patches, and stitch in straight lines where possible. For the Churn Dash block (Chapter 4), for example, you would start by assembling the triangles and rectangles into squares, join these squares into rows, and finally join the three rows of squares together. However, if you are sewing a block in which it is necessary to stitch into a corner to set in a piece, pin the first two edges to be stitched together (the two that create the corner) and sew up to the seam allowance (not to the edge of the fabric), then sew the third piece to one side of the angle up to the corner, pivot the fabric and continue sewing the second part of the seam.

STITCHING

Place the patches right sides together and pin, with the marked stitching lines matching up. When hand-stitching patches together, use a neat running stitch on the marked sewing lines of each piece. Place the patches to be joined right sides together and match the lines with pins. The stitching should start and end at each seam line (not the edge of the fabric, see diagram) and should always start with a small knot or back stitch and finish firmly with

PIECING ORDER FOR AMERICAN BLOCKS

Arrange the pieces of the block in the correct position.

Assemble each square.

← grain of fabric →

Sew the squares together in rows.

Join the rows to form one block.

PIECING:
Setting a Piece into a Corner

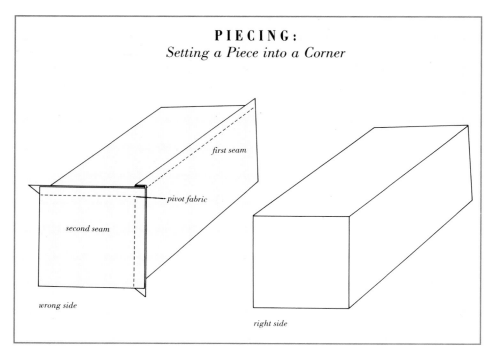

a back stitch or two to prevent the seams from coming undone. Waxing will prevent the thread from knotting to some extent. Seam allowances should be pressed to one side, to the darker side of the seam where possible. When quilted this makes stronger seams and prevents the stitches from bulging open.

MACHINE STITCHED

Patches cut with templates made for machine piecing already have the seam allowance added. Piecing order follows the same principles as for hand stitched patchwork – smaller patches into larger ones and straight lines of stitching where possible. Machine-stitched seams are stronger and can be pressed open. Place patches right sides together and guide the raw edge against the presser foot – most sewing-machines will give a ¼ in (6 mm) seam allowance. If yours does not, mark the plate on your machine parallel to the seam line and ¼ in (6 mm) from the needle using a narrow strip of masking tape and use that as a seam guide.

PIECING ANGLED SHAPES

When joining shapes that run at an angle, other than a right angle, eg, diamonds and triangles, align the stitching lines, *not* the cut edges. This makes a straight edge when the patches are opened.

MATCHING POINTS

Some blocks have a point at which four or more fabrics meet. To match these points accurately, push a pin through at the exact spot where the points are to be matched at a right angle to your stitching. Stitch up to the pin, remove carefully and stitch over the point.

Appliqué

Appliqué, from the French word to apply, is the technique of cutting out pieces of material and stitching them to a background. This was a way of extending the life of a garment or bedspread which had become worn in places, or of making expensive pieces of material go further. Various motifs, including flora and fauna were cut and stitched into elaborate de-

HANDSTITCHED AMERICAN PATCHWORK

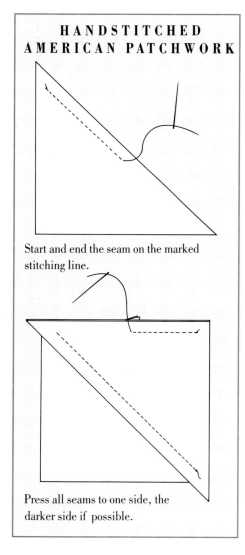

Start and end the seam on the marked stitching line.

Press all seams to one side, the darker side if possible.

MACHINE-STITCHED AMERICAN PATCHWORK

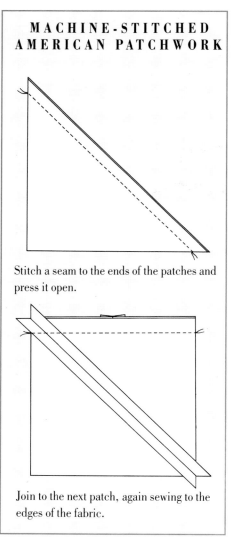

Stitch a seam to the ends of the patches and press it open.

Join to the next patch, again sewing to the edges of the fabric.

PIECING ANGLED SHAPES

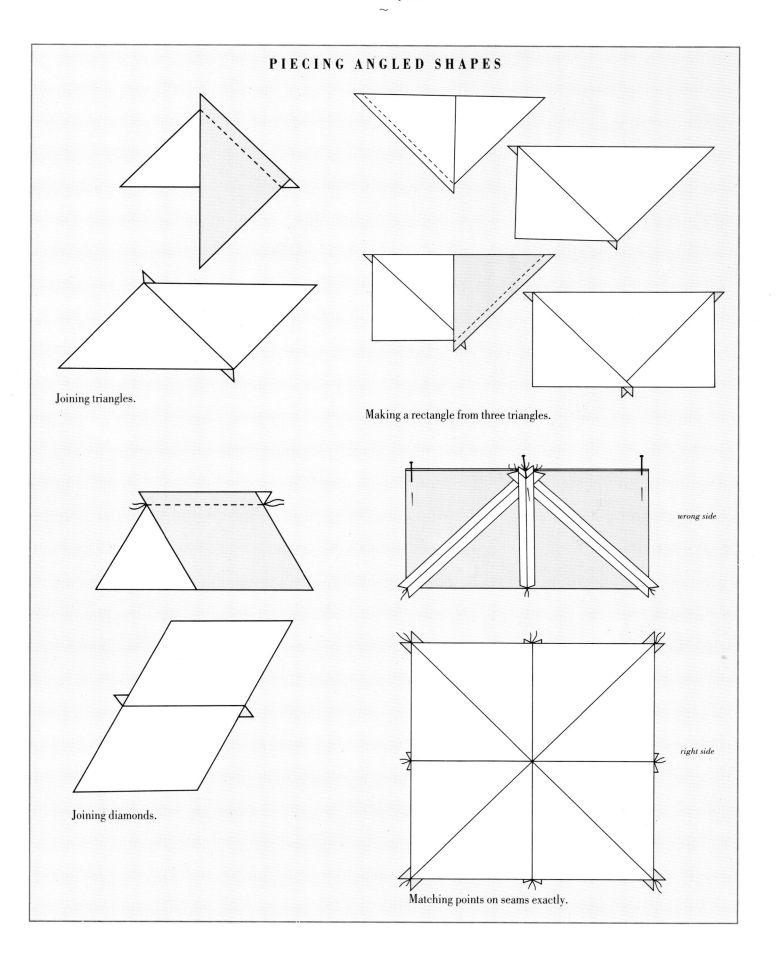

Joining triangles.

Making a rectangle from three triangles.

Joining diamonds.

wrong side

right side

Matching points on seams exactly.

LEFT The Carolina Lily Block is a combination of piecing and appliqué.

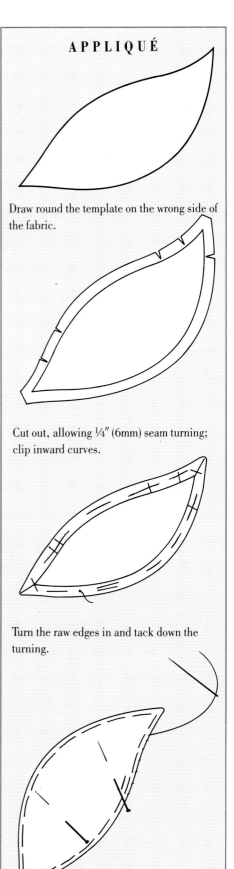

APPLIQUÉ

Draw round the template on the wrong side of the fabric.

Cut out, allowing ¼″ (6mm) seam turning; clip inward curves.

Turn the raw edges in and tack down the turning.

Pin and tack, then stitch down.

signs. Sometimes one large image was made, a tree of life for example, sometimes a series of similar repeated blocks, as in the Baltimore brides' quilts.

The technique lends itself more to pictorial designs and curved shapes than to pieced patchwork which is characterized by geometric designs and straight seams. The two techniques of appliqué and piecing were often used together in quilt designs such as the Flower Basket and the Carolina Lily.

Appliqué templates are the actual size of the piece to be applied and the seam allowance, or turning, must be added as the fabric is cut. The templates can be drawn freehand, traced from patterns or made from cut and folded paper. Place the template face down on the back of the fabric, draw round it with a fabric marker and cut out adding ¼ in (6 mm) to turn under. The raw edges of the piece must be turned under before it is pinned and stitched to the background. Clip any inward curves to facilitate turning under the edge, up to but not beyond the marked

line, turn the edge under and press. Now position the piece on the background, pin and tack (baste) if necessary, then hem down with neat stitches using a thread that matches the piece. Where several pieces are used, in a picture for example, the edge of one piece may be overlapped by the edge of another. In this case it is not necessary to turn under the raw edges of the piece to be overlapped. When the pieces have been stitched down to the background, to reduce its thickness and make quilting easier cut away the background fabric behind the piece ¼ in (6 mm) from the sewing line with a pair of sharp scissors.

Borders

If your quilt design includes a border, this must be added as part of the quilt top. Plain borders can provide an area for an elaborate quilting design or they can balance and contain the patchwork. A pieced border should complement the patchwork blocks. Try to use multiples of the measurement units that are in the quilt.

BORDERS

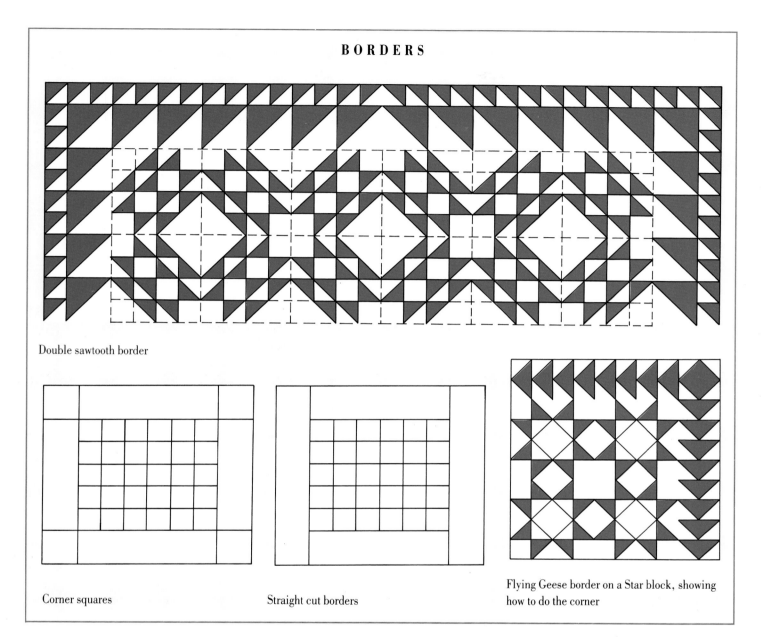

Double sawtooth border

Corner squares

Straight cut borders

Flying Geese border on a Star block, showing
how to do the corner

Search the block pattern for border ele-
ments. A border, if included, should be
an integral part of the quilt design, and
not just added to make up the size.

STRAIGHT CUT BORDERS

Cut two strips to the length of the patchwork and the desired width, plus seam
allowance, and stitch these to the sides.
Now cut two more to match the width of
the patchwork plus the added width of
the long strips and join these to the top
and the bottom.

CORNER SQUARES

This is a simple but effective border. Cut

two strips to match the long sides of the
patchwork and two strips to match the
short sides, to the desired width plus
seam allowance, and cut four squares the
sides of which match the width of the
border. Join two strips to the sides of the
patchwork. Now add the corner squares
to each end of the remaining strips and
stitch these along the top and bottom, ensuring that the joins match.

MITRED CORNERS

For a border with mitred corners proceed
as follows: cut the border strips to the desired width. The length of each strip
should equal the length of the side of the

patchwork, plus a generous allowance for
the width of the border, which will allow
for the mitres. Join the borders to the
patchwork right sides together, and stop
the stitching at the seam allowance at each
corner. Place the quilt top right side down
on a flat surface and fold one border over
another and draw a straight line from the
inner corner at an angle of 45° to the
border. Reverse the positions of the
borders and repeat. With the right sides of
the borders together line up the marked
seam lines and stitch from the inner to the
outer corner. Before trimming away excess fabric, open the corner seam and press
it to ensure it lies flat.

MITRED CORNERS

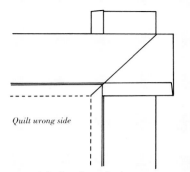

Draw a straight line from the inner corner at a 45° angle.

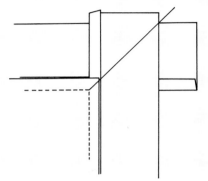

Reverse borders and repeat.

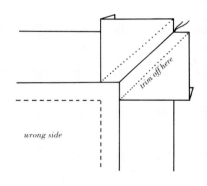

Stitch the borders together along the marked lines and press open. Trim away excess fabric.

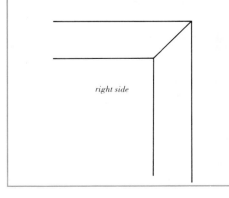

LEFT & BELOW Quilting by hand with a hoop
~

OPPOSITE Part of a Dresden Plate Block showing contour quilting.
~

Assembling the Quilt

When piecing is complete, press the quilt top well; once the wadding (batting) and backing are attached ironing is not recommended as it will flatten the filler. If the top is bigger than the widest fabric available you will have to piece the backing and wadding, both of which should be 4 in (10 cm) bigger all round than the top. To join wadding butt the edges against each other and join with herringbone stitch edge to edge to avoid a ridge. Remove any selvedges from the backing before joining to make the size you need. Lay the backing wrong side up on a flat surface (on the floor if the quilt is large) and if possible tape it down. Smooth the wadding down gently on top, then the quilt top, being careful not to pull or stretch either as this may distort the quilt. Pin all three layers together, smoothing out wrinkles from the top and bottom. Starting from the centre, tack the three layers together easing excess fabric towards the edge. Cover the quilt with a grid of stitches 4–6 in (10–15 cm) apart.

Quilting

There are various ways of securing the three layers of the quilt together.

TIE QUILTING

For a quilt with a bulky filler such as 4-oz or 6-oz wadding (batting), or as a quick way to complete your quilt, tie quilting is ideal. Using thread in a strong natural fibre such as embroidery or crochet cotton, pull it through all three layers leaving an end long enough to tie (5 in/13 cm). Stitch again over the first stitch bringing the needle up near the loose end. Tie in a reef knot not too tightly as this might cause the fabric to tear. Trim the ends, or thread them into the quilt. Tie at regular intervals over the quilt surface, about 4–6 in (10–15 cm) apart. The knots can be used as decorative features either by themselves or in conjunction with buttons, beads or French knots.

HAND-QUILTING

Hand-quilting is done with small, even running stitches through the three layers of the quilt. A close web of quilting was necessary on old quilts to prevent the raw wool or cotton filler from bunching together at one end of the quilt, but with the bonded quilt wadding available today you can do as much or as little quilting as you like. Close quilting is still admired for the added texture it gives.

To hand quilt, take a length (about 16 in/40 cm) of single quilting thread and run it through bees wax, to strengthen the thread and help to prevent it knotting. Start with a knot and come up from the back of the quilt, tug the thread until the knot pops through the back. Try to keep stitches as even as possible; this is more important than their size. Quilting can be done on your lap, or you may prefer to use a hoop or frame. A quilting frame is a large and expensive item and if you have one you are probably already an experienced quilter. More accessible to the beginner is a hoop rather like an embroidery ring only larger – about 23 in (57 cm) in diameter. This may be on a stand, or can be rested against a table leaving both hands free. Keep the quilt fairly slack in the hoop and push the needle through from the top with a thimble worn on the middle finger of the sewing hand. Keep the other hand beneath the work to guide the needle back up. Expert quilters use a flat topped thimble on the lower hand, grazing the needle on the top

angle as they stitch, which ensures that each stitch has gone through all three layers. Take three to four running stitches with a rocking movement, keeping the thumb pressed down on the fabric just ahead of the stitching. To finish, tie a knot close to the last stitch and pull this through between the layers, bring the needle out at the front and cut the thread off.

Many quilt shows have demonstrations of quilting which are worth seeking out; an effective way of acquiring this skill.

QUILTING PATTERNS

Contour quilting A straightforward and traditional style of quilting, this echoes the shapes of the patches, which are outlined with a row of stitching ⅜ in (1 cm) from the seams. You can mark an even line with narrow masking tape or a fabric marker. Check on a scrap of fabric that any marks will come off.

Stencils Quilting designs form another study in themselves. Antique quilts have elaborate motifs which were marked on to the quilt top with stencils or drawn freehand by expert quilt-markers. Cables,

feathers and tulips were popular and together with geometric 'filler' patterns form highly decorative bas-relief surfaces on the quilt. Stencils are available in patchwork supply shops and can be used to mark out a quilting design. The quilt top should be marked before the three layers are assembled.

QUILTING BY MACHINE

If you plan to quilt by machine there are several points to consider. Tacking must be as thorough as for hand-quilting. Try to work out a quilting design which as far as possible runs in straight lines that do not cross. Turning a large quilt in the sewing machine is difficult; consider quilting larger items in two pieces and joining after quilting. To do this, when quilting is finished place the two halves right sides together and join through all thicknesses matching points where necessary. Trim away as much of the wadding as possible to reduce bulk, then pin a narrow strip of bias binding, matched to the backing, over the join and hem it to either side of the seam.

It is possible to buy a walking foot for some models of sewing-machine, and this attachment makes machine-quilting much easier. This is because it feeds the three layers of fabric through evenly rather than running the top layer forward, as does the standard foot, which may create small tucks. Keep the bulk of the quilt rolled up when you are not working on it and support it on the sewing-table. Mark quilting lines on the surface with a marker and try to match threads with the colour of the top where possible. Machine-quilting can be hidden in the seam. To do this press the fabric down as you work and open the seam to allow the needle to hit the centre or 'ditch' of the seam.

You can either start or finish with back stitches and clip off the threads, or pull all the threads through to the back and darn them into the quilt.

THREAD FOR MACHINE QUILTING
Use the type of thread you would normally use in your machine and match it to the quilt top where possible. Alternatively use invisible thread on top with thread to match the backing in the bobbin. The stitch length should be slightly longer (about 10–11 stitches per inch/25 mm) than for a seam.

If you have a machine that does decorative stitching, experiment with this to accent your machine quilting. A narrow

STRAIGHT BINDING

Cut the binding 2½" (6cm) wide, and the length of the quilt edge.

Fold in half along the length and press.

Quilt right side

Pin and stitch the raw edges to the quilt on the right side. Stitch ¼" (6mm) from edge.

Turn the folded edge of binding over to the wrong side of the quilt and hem it down.

ABOVE *Threads for machine quilting.*

satin stitch with a multi-coloured thread forms the decorative focus on the block centres in 'log cabin windows', for example (see Chapter 5).

Final Finishing

When quilting is complete the edges must be neatened either by turning the raw edges of the quilt top and tacking to the inside and stitching together or putting a binding around the quilt to enclose the wadding (batting) and raw edges.

STRAIGHT BINDING
If a narrow binding is folded along its length before being stitched to the edges of the quilt, this makes a folded edge to turn over and enclose the raw edges and

wadding (batting) which is easily hemmed in place. This method makes it easier to get an even width of binding, giving the quilt a more professional finish. For the sides of the quilt cut two pieces of fabric on the straight grain to the desired length by 2½ in (6 cm) wide. Fold these strips in half along their length and press. There is now one side with two raw edges and one side with a fold. Place the side with raw edges along the top side of the quilt. Pin, tack (baste) and stitch through both layers of the binding and all layers of the quilt, taking in a ¼ in (6 mm) seam allowance. Turn the folded edge of the binding over the raw edges and hem down on the back of the quilt enclosing the wadding (batting). Repeat on the opposite side. For the

CORNERS

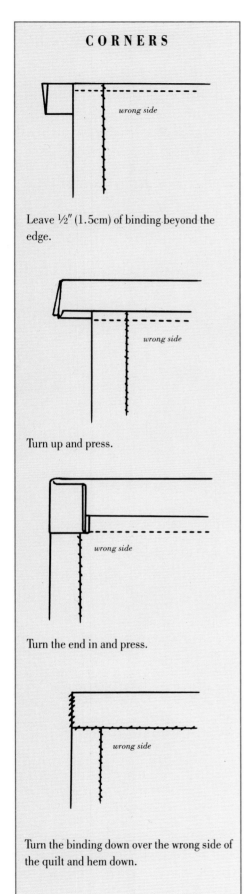

Leave ½″ (1.5cm) of binding beyond the edge.

wrong side

Turn up and press.

wrong side

Turn the end in and press.

wrong side

Turn the binding down over the wrong side of the quilt and hem down.

BIAS BINDING

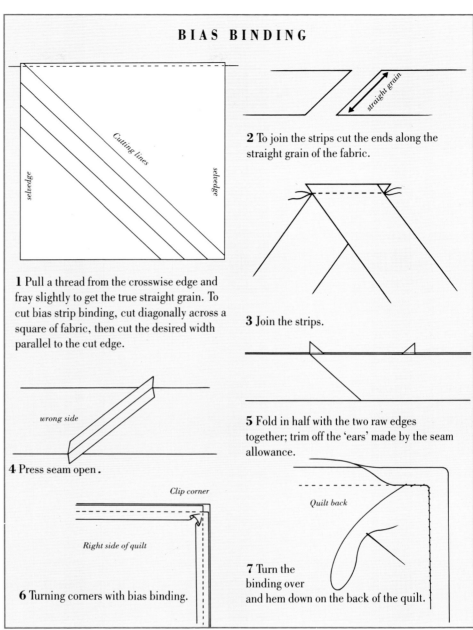

1 Pull a thread from the crosswise edge and fray slightly to get the true straight grain. To cut bias strip binding, cut diagonally across a square of fabric, then cut the desired width parallel to the cut edge.

2 To join the strips cut the ends along the straight grain of the fabric.

3 Join the strips.

4 Press seam open.

5 Fold in half with the two raw edges together; trim off the 'ears' made by the seam allowance.

6 Turning corners with bias binding.

7 Turn the binding over and hem down on the back of the quilt.

top and bottom leave ½ in (1.5 cm) of binding extending beyond the corners and neaten by turning in or mitring before final hemming.

BIAS BINDING
If a bias strip binding is used, it can be stitched all round the edges of the quilt continuously as the stretch in the bias cut of the material will ease round the corners. Measure the perimeter of your quilt and cut across the diagonal of the binding fabric in 2½ in (6.5 cm) wide strips. Join together enough pieces to accommodate the desired length using diagonal seams.

The bias strip is fairly stretchy so allow for this when estimating the length you need. Seam the ends of the binding pieces together to make a continuous ring. Press seams open then fold the binding in half with the wrong sides innermost. At this point you may trim off the 'ears' created by the seams. Pin the raw edges of the binding to the edge of the quilt on the top side. Tack and stitch with a ¼ in (6 mm) seam allowance. At the corners clip into the binding, but not past the seam allowance, to turn the corner more easily. Continue stitching around the corner. Turn the binding over the raw edge and hem.

Chapter Three

ENGLISH PATCHWORK

~

Granny's Garden

~

" *T*he first quilt pattern printed in an American periodical was an English hexagon patchwork design which appeared in the January 1835 issue of Godey's Lady's Book. "

Penny McMorris, Catalogue to the 1986 Quilt Art Touring Exhibition.

Although it is more time-consuming than other methods, English patchwork does have certain advantages. It is possible to fit interlocking shapes together accurately, and if they are firmly stitched together, the result is a strong fabric. Curved pieces can be made, as in the Dresden Plate quilt, and then appliquéd on to a background. Of course, unless they are going to be combined with other shapes, it is a waste of time to stitch squares or rectangles together using this method. The American technique would be more suitable, and much less time-consuming.

Design

Try out different design layouts for hexagons, stars, diamonds and triangles on isometric graph paper. These shapes can be used singly or in combination. Isometric paper is marked out in a grid of triangles, and can also be used for making the papers which are tacked (basted) into the fabric patches, and for tracing accurate templates. Sort scrap fabrics into colour groups or tone values so that you can impose some order on your designs, or use a common fabric as a background or border. Although many English quilts are one-patch designs, that is, one shape is repeated, you can still work on the quilt in units rather than allowing it to grow so big as to be unwieldy.

DESIGNS ON ISOMETRIC GRAPH PAPER

Combining shapes over an isometric grid.

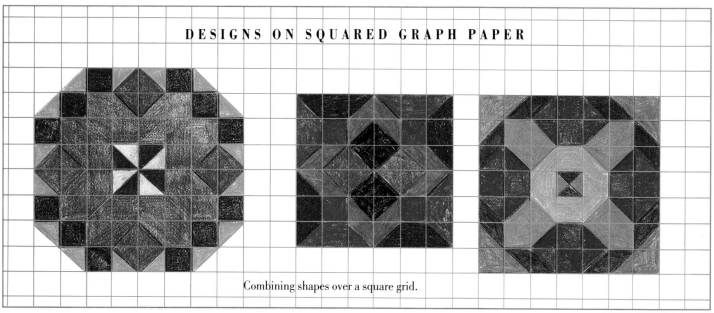

DESIGNS ON SQUARED GRAPH PAPER

Combining shapes over a square grid.

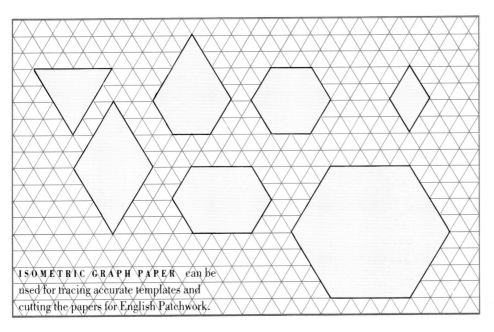

ISOMETRIC GRAPH PAPER can be used for tracing accurate templates and cutting the papers for English Patchwork.

SKETCH PLAN OF QUILT
on isometric graph paper

A sketch plan of the whole quilt can be made on isometric graph paper to provide a key to the layout and positioning of colour groups, dark and light areas and borders.

Grandmother's Flower Garden

Made of 19th-century dress cottons, this quilt is a straightforward interpretation of the flower garden design. Simple rosettes made of seven hexagons float in a field of acid green sprigged cotton which is also used for the border and backing. The restricted colour scheme of reddish browns and blue printed cotton give the quilt a calm and restful appeal. Striped and checked fabrics have been used in some of the rosettes and these form interesting focal points in the otherwise even texture of the surface. The quilting outlines the hexagons. Quilts with an 'antique' look are enjoying popularity at the moment; one American fabric manufacturer has revived some of the old dress prints from this era, and it is possible to buy preparations to artificially fade new quilts. Certainly, to attempt to reproduce a quilt like this would require careful selection of fabrics in a muted colour range, but the hexagonal shape is the least demanding in terms of sewing technique, so perseverance would be more important than skill in the production of such a quilt.

MATERIALS REQUIRED
Each rosette takes one piece of fabric 12 in × 8 in (30 cm × 20 cm) and a piece for the centre 4 in × 4 in (10 cm × 10 cm). There are 115 rosettes in the quilt top and 34 half rosettes around the edges.

▪ For the background hexagons: 4½ yd (metres) of 45 in (115 cm) fabric.

▪ Border and backing: 7 yd (metres).

▪ Wadding (batting): the finished size of the quilt top, plus 4 in (10 cm) all round.

▪ A hexagon template with 1–1½ in (3–4 cm) sides.

▪ Paper for the backing papers.

Using the template, cut the papers and cover them with fabric, then make up the rosettes (Chapter 2). If you make up all the rosettes first, then join them to the background fabric hexagons, you will

*ABOVE Grandmother's
Flower Garden quilt*

~

*RIGHT A sample piece of
Grandmother's Flower
Garden made in
contemporary fabrics.*

~

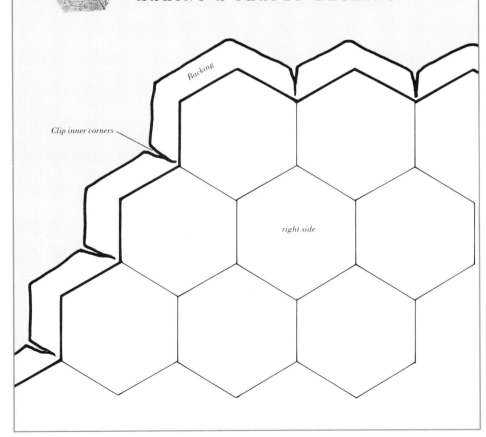

Granny's Garden

This quilt, made with hexagons using the English method of piecing, successfully bridges the gap separating contemporary quilt-making and the traditional Victorian mosaic quilts. It is composed of double rosettes of hexagons in mainly orange and earth tones, each with a yellow centre. These rosettes make creative use of the fabric prints, giving the quilt the same feel as an exquisite antique glass paperweight. Stripes radiate from and circle round the rosette centres. Printed squares set at random angles within some of the hexagons give the quilt a sense of movement, and the framing and placing of flower and paisley motifs demonstrate the skilled use of window templates. There is enough deliberate manipulation of tonal values in the centrally placed circle of lighter rosettes to give the design order, but the variety of fabrics used keeps the eye moving around the surface of the quilt

ABOVE Back view of Grandmother's Flower Garden quilt using contemporary fabrics.

~

MAKING A SHAPED BACKING

Backing

Clip inner corners

right side

have more control over the placement of colours. Alternatively, if you begin connecting the rosettes when you have completed several, a more random arrangement can develop. Once a hexagon is surrounded completely, the paper can be removed and re-used several times. It appears that the edges of this quilt have been cut through the patchwork. in order to straighten them and attach the border, but other possibilities are suggested in chapter one. When the patchwork top and border is complete, assemble with the backing and wadding (batting) and quilt by outlining the hexagons. Finish with a narrow binding made from the border fabric, or turn the edges of the backing and border together and slip hem.

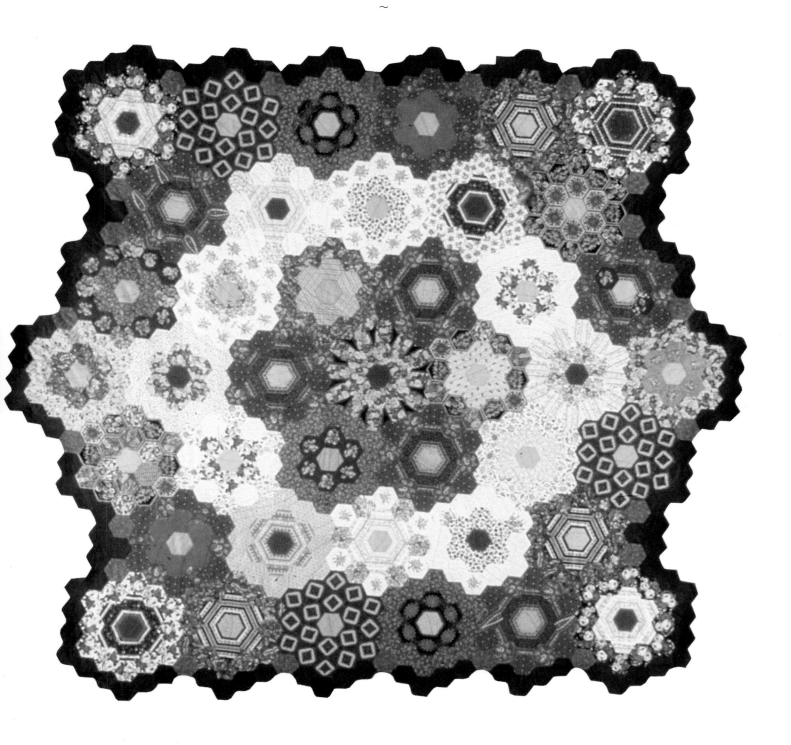

to investigate detail within that order. The final touch is in the border: by allow–ing the hexagons themselves to frame the quilt, the maker has not only dispensed with the problems of straightening the edge, but has projected her interpretation of the hexagon into contemporary focus. The quilting is done in bold, even stitches in hand-embroidery cotton. There is no wadding (batting) in the quilt.

MAKING A SHAPED BACKING

To shape the backing to the outer hexa–gons press the outer edges of the patch–work and carefully remove the papers. Cut the backing fabric, 1½ in (3.5 cm) larger than the quilt top all round, and tack (baste) the top and backing together with wrong sides facing. Trim the backing fabric round the shaped edge ⅜ in (9 mm) larger all round. Clip the inner corners on

ABOVE Granny's
Garden Quilt.
~

the backing fabric so that when turned in it will lie flat against the back of the patch–work. Turn in the backing so that the folded edges of the patchwork and back–ing match up, pin, tack (baste) and slip hem the edges together. Quilt and remove tacking.

RIGHT *Stars and Hexagons quilt top.*
~

Stars and Hexagons Quilt Top

This quilt top, which has never been backed or quilted, was made in the late 19th century. It is a fine example of the decorative mosaic quilts made from silks and satins by middle-class women. These quiltmakers were not working from necessity but rather to demonstrate their skill, as the elaborate design composed of hexagons, diamonds and tiny triangles illustrates. The materials that were used, and the intricate piecing, served to demonstrate the wealth and leisure that was enjoyed by the Victorian middle classes. The hexagons were made from gentlemen's ties, whilst the diamonds and triangles were silk offcuts from fashionable silk dresses of the day.

RIGHT & BELOW *These samples show how different shapes can be combined in English patchwork. Isometric graph paper was used to plan the designs and for the backing papers.*
~

Each unit is a hexagon composed of a six-pointed star of diamonds surrounded by six hexagons and six small triangles. These are placed in circles which radiate around the centre motif, displaying a fine degree of planning. The overall effect is that of a panel of luminous marquetry, the texture of the fabric reflecting the light as would a well-polished piece of wood.

This quilt has been included rather as an example of how shapes and patterned fabrics can be successfully combined together using English piecing than to be reproduced exactly, which would be very costly to do. However, a fine cotton or cotton lawn would be a far more manageable fabric to work with for such a project, as silk has a tendency to be very slippery and to fray badly, causing problems when dealing with the small triangles.

Dresden Plate Quilt

The use of a combination of summer dress prints and yellow and cream fabric in this quilt conjures up the images of bygone summers. Made in the 1930s in the Dresden plate pattern, the pointed-corner segments suggest the sunray figure popular in the Art Deco style of the period. Each of the 'plates' is made up of a random collection of prints in soft pinks and blues, but they are unified by these corner segments and the centre detail in a consistent yellow print. This appears again in the elegant border detail which echoes the rounded petal shapes from the circular plate motif. The cream base squares are joined leaving a narrow gap which results in a pleasing, regular arrangement overall. The quilting in the intersections between the blocks reflects the circular theme.

MATERIALS REQUIRED
Based on 45 in (115 cm) wide fabric –

▮ For each 'plate': sixteen fabrics (see template for sizes).
▮ Corner segments, circles and border: 2 yd (metres).
▮ Foundation fabric: 5 yd (metres).
▮ Backing fabric: 6 yd (metres).
▮ Wadding (batting): 100 in × 100 in (250 cm × 250 cm).

MAKING THE DRESDEN PLATE BLOCKS

Trace the template patterns A and B and make card templates. For each 'plate' cut 16 A papers and 4 B papers. Pin the papers to the fabric and cut out as described in Chapter 2. Before tacking (basting) the fabric to the paper template A, stitch a gathering thread round the curved end of the segment. To do this stitch a row of small running stitches starting from a knot, then pull this up to gather the fabric, fitting the fabric over the paper to give a smooth curve, and fasten off with 2 or 3 back stitches. Start the tacking stitches at the narrow end of the segment (point X on the diagram). When you get back to the opposite corner of the narrow edge finish off the tacking.

Do not fold the fabric over the narrow edge as this will be covered by the centre circle. When all 20 of the segments (templates A and B) have been covered, whipstitch together down the long straight sides

ABOVE: Dresden Plate quilt.
~

positioning the pointed segment shapes at each quarter point of the plate. When all segments are joined in a circle, press well with a steam iron or dry iron and damp cloth to put a firm crease around the outer edge, then carefully remove the tacking (basting) and papers. Leave the gathering stitches in as this will help to keep the seam allowance folded down. At this point the outer edge can be tacked (basted) to hold the turning under.

THE CENTRE

For the centre motif the pieces are joined with a small running stitch as in hand-stitched American patchwork, rather than stitched over papers. Trace templates C and D, transfer the shape to card and cut out carefully. For each centre cut one shape C and four shape D. Draw round the templates on the wrong side of the fabric and

TEMPLATES FOR THE DRESDEN PLATE QUILT

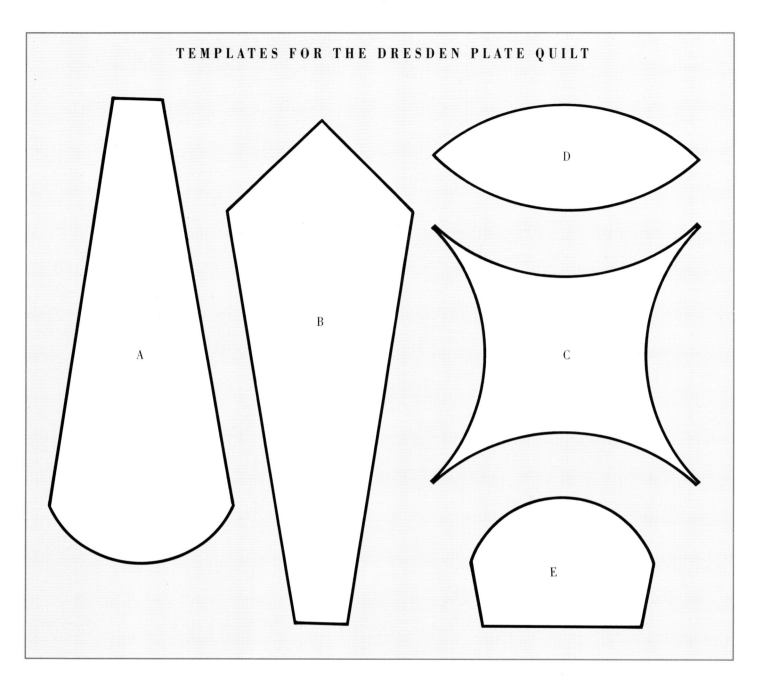

cut out adding ¼ in (6 mm) seam allowance. Before stitching the pieces together clip the curved sides of shape C from the edge of the fabric just up to the seam allowance (about ³/₁₆ in/4 mm). Place the fabrics right sides together and stitch, along the lines marked round the templates, easing the curves together. Press the seams towards the outside of the circle. When all four of shape D have been stitched to shape C turn the outer edge in by a ¼ in (6 mm) to make the circular central motif. To give the centre piece a smooth curve, gather the outside edge then pin a 4 in (10 cm)

diameter circle of paper to the back of the centre piece. Pull up the gathering thread, tack (baste) the fabric over the paper then press with a steam iron, or damp cloth and dry iron, to form a smooth crease around the outer edge. Now take out the tacking (basting) stitches and remove the paper, but leave the gathering stitches in.

Place the circle of fabric in the centre of the 'plate', pin and stitch down with small overcast stitches in a thread which matches the circle fabric. Cut a 16-in (40-cm) square of the foundation fabric and position the 'plate' in the centre with the pointed seg-

ments running vertically and horizontally (see picture). Smooth down, pin, tack (baste) and stitch down with a neutral-coloured thread which blends in with the fabric colours.

FINISHING THE BLOCK

Remove all tacking (basting) and press. In order to reduce the bulk and to make quilting easier, the foundation fabric is removed behind the applied 'plate' motif. Turn the block over, and with small sharp scissors cut away the foundation fabric ¼ in (6 mm) from the stitching line.

PREPARING PATCHES FOR THE DRESDEN PLATE QUILT

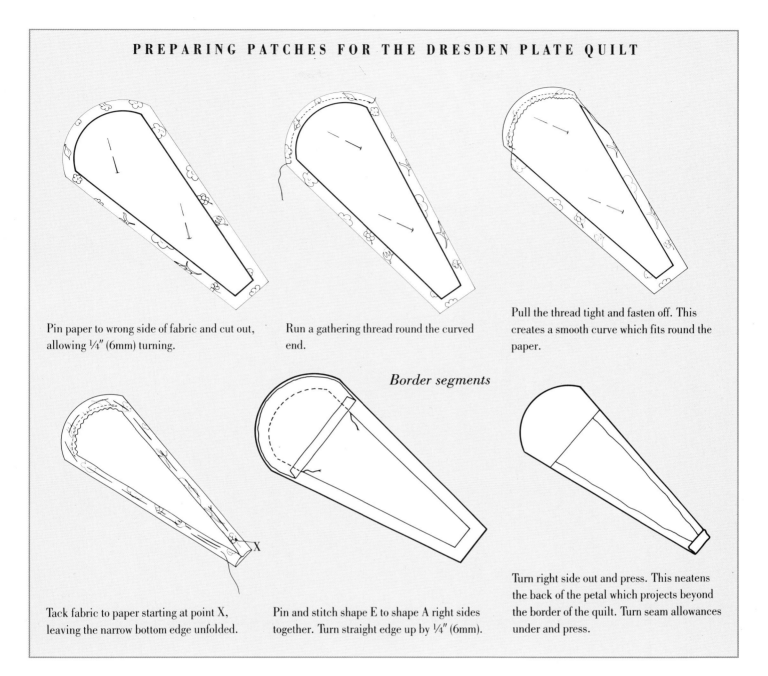

Pin paper to wrong side of fabric and cut out, allowing ¼" (6mm) turning.

Run a gathering thread round the curved end.

Pull the thread tight and fasten off. This creates a smooth curve which fits round the paper.

Border segments

Tack fabric to paper starting at point X, leaving the narrow bottom edge unfolded.

Pin and stitch shape E to shape A right sides together. Turn straight edge up by ¼" (6mm).

Turn right side out and press. This neatens the back of the petal which projects beyond the border of the quilt. Turn seam allowances under and press.

MAKING UP THE QUILT TOP

When all 20 blocks have been completed, join them together in rows of 4 blocks across the quilt and 5 blocks down, taking ¼ in (6 mm) seam allowance. Press the seams open.

THE BORDER

Cut the border strips 4¾ in (12 cm) wide and stitch to the sides and the top and bottom as for straight cut borders (see Chapter 2). The petal decoration is applied after quilting. Assemble the three layers of the quilt and quilt by hand or machine,

then round off the corners and bind the edges with a bias strip binding (Chapter 2).

PETAL BORDERS

To make segments for the petal border, place template A onto the wrong side of the fabric and mark a line all round with a fabric marker. Cut out the fabric to include ¼ in (6 mm) seam allowance. Using template E, mark and cut a piece of fabric to neaten the back of the petal where it projects over the edge of the border. Place A and E right sides together, turn up ¼ in

(6 mm) on the straight side of shape E, and stitch round the curve on the marked line. Turn inside out and push the seams out to create a smooth curve. Press turnings to the wrong side making sure that the petal measures 4¾ in (12 cm) from the curved end to the narrow straight end. Make enough petals to fit round the edge of the quilt and appliqué them to the border by hand, leaving the curved, neatened edge projecting over the edge of the quilt (refer to the illustration). On the quilt illustrated, there are 23 petals down each side, 19 on the top and 18 on the bottom.

Chapter Four

AMERICAN
PATCHWORK

~

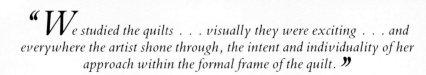

" *W* e studied the quilts . . . visually they were exciting . . . and
everywhere the artist shone through, the intent and individuality of her
approach within the formal frame of the quilt. "

Patricia Cooper & Norman Bradley Buferd, Introduction to *The Quilters: Women and Domestic Art.*

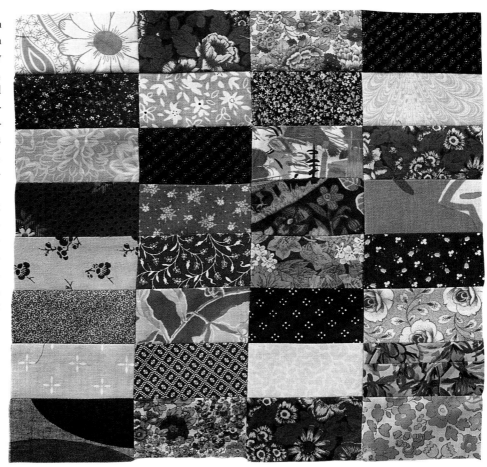

The first quilts made by the American pioneers were designed more for warmth than beauty. In the harsh winters every available resource had to be conserved and, where possible, re-cycled. Clothes and bedclothes were used and re-used, including being made into the first crazy quilts – a haphazard arrangement of fabric scraps stitched together and filled with anything, often more re-cycled fabrics such as blankets, that would insulate from the cold.

Despite the scarcity of fabrics it was not long before these early quilt-makers began to impose some order on the arrangement of colour and shapes. Simple one-patch designs such as Bricks or Hit and Miss were produced. These quilts could still make full use of available scraps but had an element of design.

The early settlers had limited living and working space, and they solved this problem by building their patchworks in units, or 'blocks'. Each block could be made individually and stacked away until there were enough to stitch together into a large sheet of patchwork to make up the quilt top. When 20 or 30 blocks were complete, the top was often quickly assembled and quilted as a cooperative effort at the 'quilting bee'.

Simple repeated designs were developed by folding squares of paper into first four, then nine equal parts, which were then sub-divided into geometric shapes. These were the beginnings of the block design, the unit on which American pieced patchwork is based. Made up in fabric, blocks can be used in a variety of different ways.

When blocks are placed edge to edge, secondary designs appear adding complexity to apparently simple block designs.

The blocks can be separated by strips of fabric, forming a lattice effect (sashing) over the quilt. This was often used on album quilts where each block is different and putting them edge to edge would result in a confusion of different shapes.

Set 'on point', the square blocks appear as diamonds. The edges of the quilt are filled with triangles to make up the square or rectangular shape.

Two or more block designs can be used together, which can create some intriguing

LEFT An Amish quilt, made to a design referred to as Churn Dash or Monkey Wrench outside Amish communities.

~

ABOVE & RIGHT Early American patchwork patterns like Bricks and Hit and Miss made full use of all available scraps of fabric.

~

secondary patterns; and a plain block used in conjunction with a patchwork block will provide an appropriate surface for elaborate quilting. Blocks are categorized by the number of equal parts into which they are divided. Four-patch and nine-patch are the most common, but there are numerous five- and seven-patch blocks. To determine which category a block falls into, impose a grid over the design. This will also help when deciding on the order of piecing; the rule is to start with the smallest pieces and work in straight lines where possible.

The colour and tonal values used in the block can radically affect its appearance. Decide which part of the block is to be

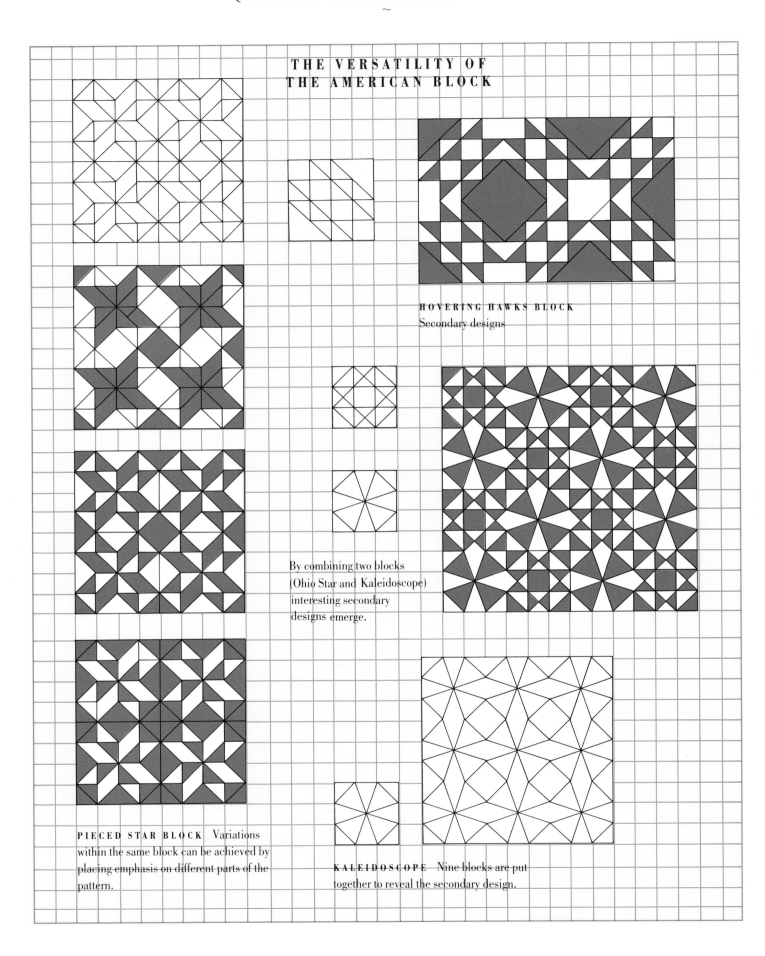

THE VERSATILITY OF
THE AMERICAN BLOCK

HOVERING HAWKS BLOCK
Secondary designs

By combining two blocks
(Ohio Star and Kaleidoscope)
interesting secondary
designs emerge.

PIECED STAR BLOCK Variations
within the same block can be achieved by
placing emphasis on different parts of the
pattern.

KALEIDOSCOPE Nine blocks are put
together to reveal the secondary design.

emphasized and use the strongest coloured fabrics on those shapes. Try shading in several versions of the same block in light, medium and dark before deciding on the position of the fabrics. Always put at least four blocks together in these drawings to reveal the secondary patterns. Some secondary patterns, eg the kaleidoscope, need at least six blocks together to show the full effect.

The basic principles of the repeat block provide a versatile way to approach quilt design. Even when simply reproducing a traditional pattern, variation and individuality can be achieved by your choice of fabrics, use of borders, and way of setting the blocks. Traditional blocks can be developed, or new ones invented within a basic grid. In the examples of block designs illustrated in this chapter, different approaches to design using the repeat block are explored.

ABOVE Castle Walls Quilt. Although each block in this quilt is the same pattern they look very different when emphasis is placed on different shapes in the block.
~
TOP LEFT Jack in the Box.
~
ABOVE LEFT Bear's Paw.
~

ALBUM QUILT WITH LATTICE STRIPS

*ABOVE Amish Churn
Dash quilt, detail.*
~

Amish Quilts

The Amish quilt-makers are notable for the graphic simplicity of their quilt designs. Working within the confines of their religious beliefs, which prescribe conformity to the 'plain' life-style and exclude any form of over-decoration including a one-time ban on patterned fabrics, they have created a stunning quilt style, recongnizable by the juxtaposing of pure colours combined with sombre browns, blues and black. Claims have been made that the abstract geometry of Amish quilts has played a significant part in the development of contemporary fine art.

The quilts are also renowned for their fine quilting, often using elaborate motifs such as rose, tulip, feather and cable. Today, antique Amish quilts are highly prized by collectors.

The Amish quilt illustrated here combines two blocks set on point. The patchwork block, sometimes known as Churn Dash, is a straightforward nine-patch and alternates with plain, closely quilted squares and triangles. A black band encloses the blocks, and the quilt is edged by a broad border in the same fabric as the plain background squares. The quilt is made in cotton and dates from the late 19th century.

Amish Churn Dash Quilt

Size 80 in × 70 in (203 cm × 178 cm)

MATERIALS REQUIRED
Fabric quantities based on 45 in (115 cm) wide fabric –
■ For the border and plain blocks: 3½ yd (metres).
■ Backing fabric: 5 yd (metres).
■ Wadding (batting): the finished size of the quilt plus 4 in (10 cm) all round.
■ Blocks: use the templates you make to calculate fabric amounts (see Chapter 2).

MAKING THE QUILT TOP
Refer to Chapter 2 for the quilt layout and order of piecing. Being a simple nine-patch, this block design is one of the easiest and quickest to construct. As the blocks alternate with plain squares, construction of the top will be speeded up. Use the layout in Chapter 2 and if necessary make any adjustments to the size of the blocks and borders. You may like to substitute one of the other block designs from the collection illustrated. Draw up the block on graph paper to the correct size and make templates. At this stage you must decide whether you are sewing by hand or machine as this will affect the templates.

The only difficulty with using the blocks set on point is in deciding which way to place the grain of the fabric. Make the blocks up with the fabric grain parallel to the sides of each block, and cut the side and corner triangles to be consistent with the blocks. Borders cut on the bias would cause too many problems with stretching and fitting, so cut them straight. This will help to contain the centre patchwork section. It is better to be flexible over the way you cut the fabric than to cause yourself extra problems by sticking rigidly to the rules. When all the blocks are made refer to the illustration and stitch them together in rows with a triangle at each end and on the corners. Stitch the rows together, matching the points between blocks. Before stitching on the borders run a line of stay stitching, that is, a straight line of running stitch, all round the edge of the patchwork to prevent it

stretching. Do this within the seam allowance so it will not show when the borders are attached. When the top is complete, assemble with the wadding (batting) and backing, and quilt and finish in the usual way (see Chapter 2).

Pinwheel Cot Quilt

A popular way of planning a scrap quilt is to use a common background fabric. In this small quilt, a plain, lavender-coloured cotton provides a uniform background to a variety of different patterned fabrics. It also unifies the design. The design of the block is a variation of the traditional Clay's Choice. (The comparison is made visually in the diagram below.) The blocks are made in such a way that when they are set edge to edge, they provide a secondary pattern which then turns the pinwheel

PINWHEEL BLOCKS

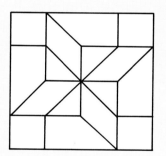

Clay's Choice – the traditional block.

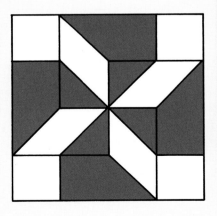

A variation used in pinwheel cot quilt. The width of the border strips is half that of each square in the block grid.

blades in opposite directions, giving the impression of spiralling movement. The plain shapes connecting the blocks are emphasized with machine quilting. The border of patterned strips is shaded through dark and light colours running gradually together. The edge of the quilt is finished with a patchwork bias binding. Quilting is done by machine using a narrow satin stitch in decorative embroidery thread, and the centre of each block is tied with a knot of hand-embroidery cotton.

The block size is 8 in (20 cm), and the border strips are 1 in × 3 in (2.5 cm × 8 cm). The overall size of the quilt is 30 in × 39 in (76 cm × 99 cm).

MATERIALS REQUIRED

Based on 45 in (115 cm) wide fabric –
■ For the blocks: 24 pieces of patterned fabric each 9 in × 6 in (23cm × 15 cm).
■ For the background: ¾ yd (metre) of plain fabric.
■ Backing: 1½ yd (metre).
■ 2 oz wadding (batting).
■ Machine-embroidery thread. Madeira shaded, colour number 2103, one 500-metre reel was used on this quilt, though any other shaded or plain thread to your own taste can be used.
■ For the border: small pieces of fabric from your scrap bag.
■ Draw and make the templates for the blocks. Three shapes are required: a square, a triangle and a rhomboid.

CUTTING OUT

Each block requires two patterned fabrics and the plain background fabric.

From the first patterned fabric cut four rhomboids. When cutting out, note that the rhomboid shape is not symmetrical so the template must be placed face down on the wrong side of the fabric.

From the second patterned fabric cut four squares.

From the plain fabric cut four squares and eight triangles.

PIECING

Follow the order of piecing outlined above. Join the blocks together 3 across and 4 down.

ABOVE Pinwheel cot quilt.

~

THE BORDER

Each strip in the border is half as wide as one of the grid squares in the block, so eight strips fit along one side of the block.

Make a template the correct width for your block and the desired length. For the 8 in (20 cm) block, the strips are 1 in × 3 in (2.5 cm × 8 cm) finished size. The sides of the corner squares measure the same as the long sides of the border strips.

Piece the border strips: 24 strips for each of the shorter edges and 32 for each

of the longer edges. Add the corner squares to each end of the shorter borders. Stitch the borders to the longer sides first, then to the shorter sides, taking care to match the points at the corners.

QUILTING

Mark the quilting lines in the plain areas between the blocks, ¾ in (2 cm) from the seams, with a fabric marker. Assemble the quilt top, wadding (batting) and backing and tack (baste) thoroughly. Stitch along the marked lines to quilt, first with straight stitch and then with a narrow satin stitch (about number 2 on the sewing

PIECING ORDER

NB: Seam allowances are not shown.

Make up 8 rectangles – 4 from 2 squares and 4 from 1 rhomboid and 2 triangles.

Stitch the rectangles together to form 4 quarters.

Make ¼ blocks into ½ blocks, then stitch the final seam up the centre.

TEMPLATE FOR PATCHWORK BIAS BINDING

The seam allowance has been added to the template.

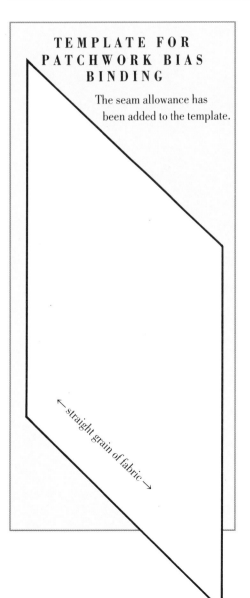

straight grain of fabric

machine) in decorative thread. Satin stitch over the join between the border and the blocks. Quilt round and between the patterned squares with a matching thread in the ditch of the seams. Tie a knot at the centre of each block with embroidery thread to match the patterned fabric.

PIECED BIAS BINDING

The bias binding is also patchwork, rather than a continuous length in one fabric. To make the patchwork bias binding, trace the template (the seam allowance has been added to the template so do not add it when cutting fabric). Now measure the perimeter of your quilt and cut enough pieces of different fabrics to give you this length. (Plan the fabrics and colours before you cut.) Remember that the bias binding is fairly stretchy, so allow for this. Seam the pieces together on the straight grain edges (ie, the short sides), taking ¼ in (6 mm) seam allowance, and join them into a continuous ring. Press all the seams open, then press the binding in half along its length with the wrong side innermost. It is now double, with two raw edges on one side and a fold on the other. Trim off the seam allowance ends that project beyond the raw edges. Now attach the binding to the quilt (see Chapter 2).

PATCHWORK BIAS BINDING

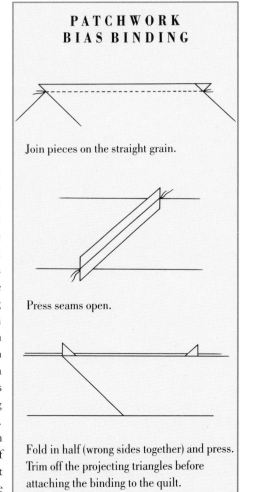

Join pieces on the straight grain.

Press seams open.

Fold in half (wrong sides together) and press. Trim off the projecting triangles before attaching the binding to the quilt.

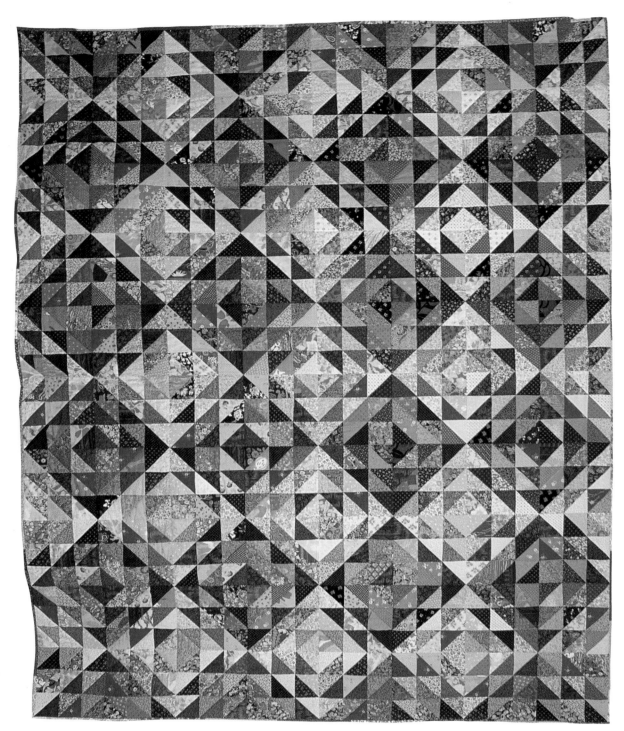

Triangles Scrap Quilt

An extensive collection of scrap fabrics goes to make up this simple quilt constructed from triangles. The block is a nine-patch made up of 18 triangles and the important element in the design is the placement of the light, medium and dark fabrics. Although the block is split diagonally into a dark side and light side, there is a variety of dark and medium tones in the dark side and three dark fabrics are included in the light side. This gives the quilt a shimmering, moving quality when the blocks are put together in fours to make the large dark and light diamonds.

The quilt is machine-pieced and quilted, with 2 oz terylene wadding (batting), and finished with straight patchwork binding.

ABOVE Triangles scrap quilt.

~

MATERIALS REQUIRED
Based on 45 in (115 cm) wide fabric (approximate measurements) –
For the blocks:
▌2 yd (metre) light
▌1 yd (metre) medium } toned fabrics.
▌3 yd (metre) dark

TRIANGLES SCRAP QUILT BLOCK

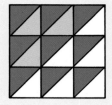

A single block made up of
6 light, 3 medium and 9 dark triangles.

4 blocks together.

16 blocks together show the full effect.

For the backing: 6 yd (metre).
∎2 oz wadding (batting).

The template is a right-angle triangle based on a 3½ in × 3½ in (9 cm × 9 cm) square. Make the template for hand or machine piecing, adjusting the size if desired. When piecing the block, refer to the diagram for placement of the fabric tones. Make 80 blocks. Put the blocks together in groups of four, dark sides innermost, then stitch these together to make the quilt top. Refer to the picture to stitch the blocks together. The size of the finished quilt top is 80 in × 100 in (204 cm × 255 cm).

Assemble with the wadding (batting) and backing and quilt by hand or machine.

STRAIGHT PATCHWORK BINDING
Cut lengths of fabric for the binding on the straight grain, 2½ in (6 cm) wide and 4–10 in (10–25 cm) long. Use fabric

pieces as in the quilt top. Seam the short sides of the pieces together to make four lengths, to match the top, bottom and sides, allowing extra material for neatening the ends on the final two pieces. Press the seams open, then fold the binding in half, wrong side innermost, and attach (straight binding, Chapter 2).

Light Maze

The formal structure of a dark lattice dissolves into light at the centre of this quilt. The contrast between light and dark, background and foreground is emphasized by the fragmentation of the light centre, pinpoints of which are carried to the edges of the quilt to shine through the dark grid. The principle of the repeated block has been extended beyond the regular repetition of the same shapes in the same colours. Instead, colour has been used in a fluid way, more in the manner of an abstract painting and the shapes, whilst still fitting

into a geometric structure, have been divided at the centre of the quilt to give the impression of diffused light contained by the regularity of the outer blocks. The basic block is a four-patch of asymmetrical design with no particular traditional references, and is composed of nine pieces.

I began to design the quilt by drawing the blocks together in various ways, in regular and random combinations. The final design for Light Maze uses both; all the blocks round the outside of the quilt have the 'V' shape pointing inwards. At the corners the block was re-designed to turn the corner, keeping within the four-patch framework. This regular border of blocks surrounds a random arrangement of the same blocks, but in the centre panel these have been further divided while keeping within the basic geometry of the block.

A plan of the quilt showing the layout of the blocks and the divisions in the centre

blocks, and which also gives some indication of colour, is essential for the construction of a quilt like this. As you make up the blocks this will be your key, and you should be able to pinpoint exactly where you are on it. Of course, the drawing cannot be exactly reproduced, as patterned fabrics will add texture and the quilting stitches will add depth to the final appearance. When making the quilt you may want to change a colour or shape as you work. It helps if you can pin blocks up and view them from a distance; the tonal values of fabric can seem very different than when seen close up.

COLOUR

Use of colour is often a source of anxiety for quilt-makers. A quilt is a long-term commitment and it is worth giving time to planning and experimenting with different colours before making a final decision. Try these simple exercises.

Take the full range of samples from one of the patchwork fabric suppliers and pick out all the colours from among the plains which you would like to use. Place them

LIGHT MAZE
Putting the blocks together

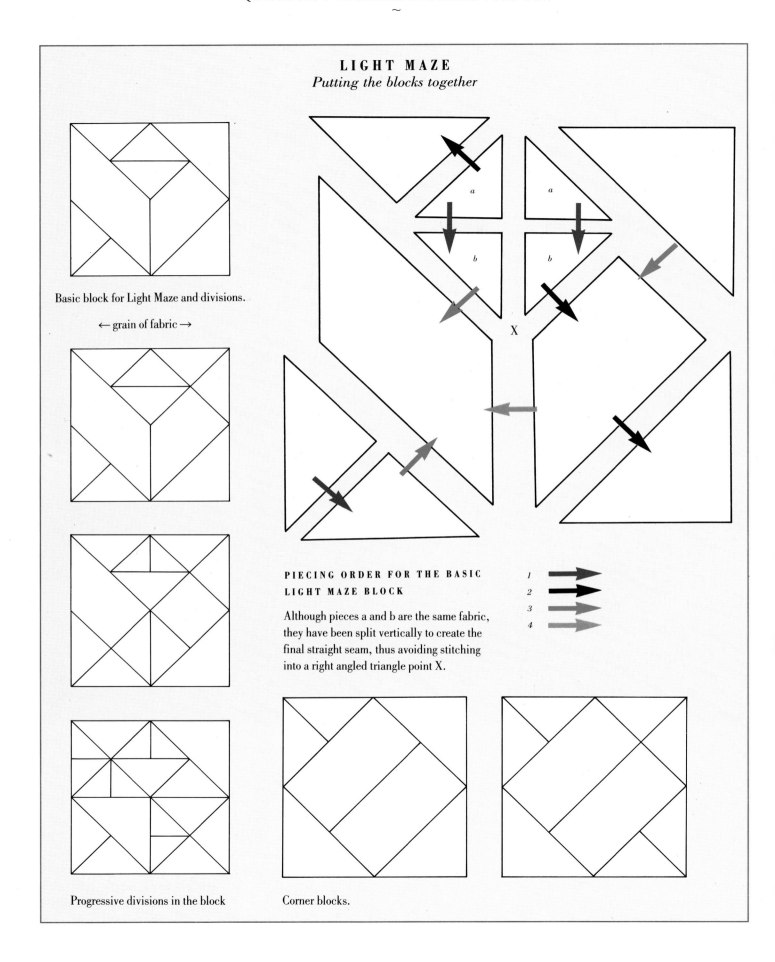

Basic block for Light Maze and divisions.

← grain of fabric →

PIECING ORDER FOR THE BASIC LIGHT MAZE BLOCK

Although pieces a and b are the same fabric, they have been split vertically to create the final straight seam, thus avoiding stitching into a right angled triangle point X.

Progressive divisions in the block

Corner blocks.

on a sheet of white paper. Now put these into groups of between three and five; try to vary the tonal values, including dark, medium and light in the groups. Now go through the patterned fabrics and put several into each group. Try altering one or two pieces from group to group, switching fabrics until you come up with some colour combinations which seem to work together. Aim for groups of between six and nine colours as a foundation on which to build. Tape the groups to sheets of paper, pin them to a board and stand away from them. You will now be able to see whether any of the fabrics will 'jump out' of the quilt because they are too vibrant. Perhaps the colours you have selected look too bland and need another fabric to accent them.

Try to devise other colour exercises for yourself. Put together colours you assume will not work and see what happens. Look at colours that have been used together in paintings or fabric designs, or even those which occur in a landscape. Try the same exercises with pieces from your fabric collection; you may only need one or two additions to achieve a pleasing colour combination.

By relaxing the formal repetitive structure of the blocks and breaking up the regular colour patterns you will be forced to make decisions which will be helped by this sort of experiment.

DESIGN

To use this approach to quilt design, first decide on a block without too many pieces; it does not have to be asymmetrical, any block that can be sub-divided will do. Think about the finished size of the quilt and draw the layout. Draw the block actual size on graph paper and then make the templates, including any extra ones needed for the sub-divisions. Mark the fabric grain on the templates.

Using your key drawing, approach the block construction as you would any traditional block – smaller pieces first and building up to larger ones. As I pieced by machine I split the two small triangles so that all the seams would be straight. In the centre of the quilt those small triangles

COLOURED DRAWING FOR LIGHT MAZE

A coloured drawing is a useful reference when experimenting with design.

are sometimes split into two colours anyway. Try to integrate plain and patterned fabrics throughout the quilt to give an even texture overall. It may help to number the blocks on the drawing and pin corresponding numbers to each completed block.

MATERIALS REQUIRED

It is difficult to predict exactly how much of each of the fabrics you will use for a quilt top like this one. For Light Maze I bought 13 plain colours and 7 prints, ¼ yd (25 cm) of each, after spending some time selecting from sample swatches. Added to these were pieces from my existing collection.

The size of this quilt is 60 in (150 cm) square which is the size of the backing and 2 oz wadding (batting) you will need.

QUILTING

The quilting was done by machine. After thorough tacking (basting) I marked the quilting lines on to the surface of the quilt using a ruler and a chalky artist's pencil. The quilting design follows the patchwork, the lines of quilting being ¾ in (9 mm) apart. If possible, when quilting on the machine use straight lines. Start and finish with about five or six back stitches and cut the threads close to the quilt surface (see machine quilting, Chapter 2).

BINDING

The binding is pieced bias strip binding, made of fabrics used in the quilt. The templates and instructions for making this are given with the Pinwheel cot quilt earlier in this chapter.

These two quilts were made using the same approach to colour and design as in Light Maze. TOP LEFT Sunshine and Shadow. In this quilt an effect of dappled sunlight was aimed for. The same block is used as in Light Maze, varying the colours, tonal values and textures in the fabric. BOTTOM LEFT Light Diamond uses a more formal approach in the organization of colour and tonal values. Within the central light diamond, pinpoints of dark can be seen and this effect is reversed in the background.

~

First Sampler quilt. A fine collection of blocks, both pieced and appliquéd, are displayed in this quilt. The variety of patterns is contained within frames of muted colours echoing the fabrics used in the block designs. The quilt is machine-pieced and hand-quilted. A sampler quilt is a good way of learning how to construct difficult block designs, and could be made by a group. Block designs can be simple or more complicated, depending on expertise, and the frames or lattice strips (sashing) will even up any differences in the block sizes, and unify the design.

~

Dictionary of Block Designs
The block designs are arranged in three sets of nine. The blocks in the first set are made only of squares and triangles and are easy to piece. The second set intro- duces another shape – the rhomboid – but with care should not present any problems. The third set of blocks is quite difficult and is recommended for the more experi- enced patchworker.

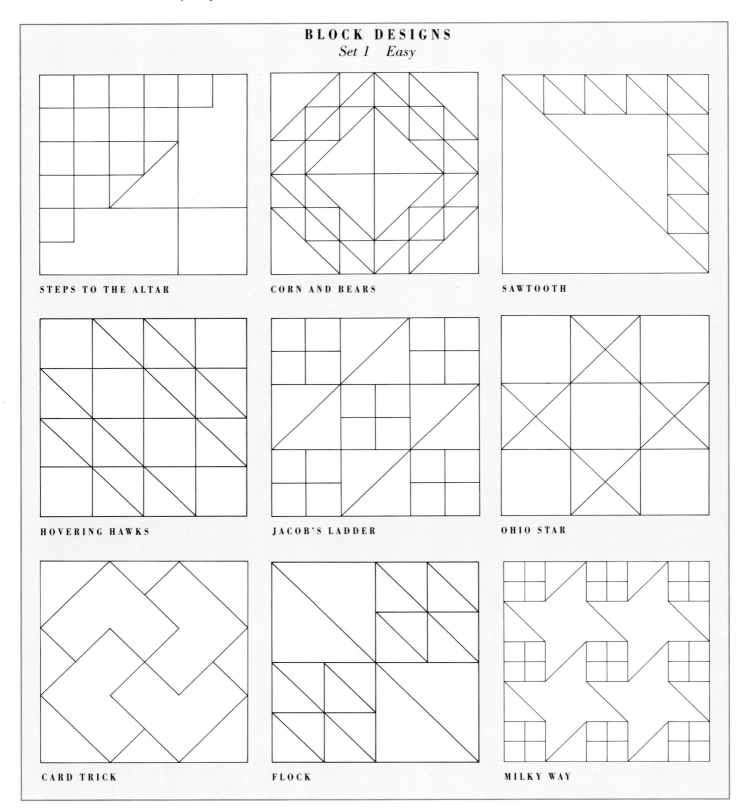

BLOCK DESIGNS
Set 1   Easy

STEPS TO THE ALTAR

CORN AND BEARS

SAWTOOTH

HOVERING HAWKS

JACOB'S LADDER

OHIO STAR

CARD TRICK

FLOCK

MILKY WAY

BLOCK DESIGNS
Set 2 Moderately easy

FARMER'S DAUGHTER

WINDBLOWN SQUARE

JACK IN THE BOX

ROLLING PINWHEEL

CLAY'S CHOICE

ARROWHEADS

PIECED STAR

GOOSE TRACKS

LILY

BLOCK DESIGNS
Set 3 Difficult

CLAWS

STAR

EASTERN STAR

STORM AT SEA

DUTCH ROSE

PIGEON TOES

DOUBLE STAR

ST LOUIS STAR

DOVE IN THE WINDOW

Courthouse Steps.

~

"*E*verything I ever learned about building and ploughing goes into these quilts."

Patricia Cooper & Norman Bradley Buferd, *The Quilters: Women and Domestic Art.*

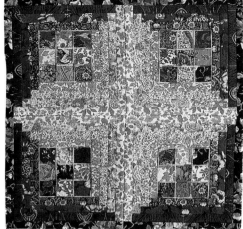

ABOVE, RIGHT & OPPOSITE
The Log Cabin block has the
potential for a wide variety of
designs: Barn Raising (this
page) and an unnamed version
(opposite).

~

Among the traditional quilt designs, log cabin ranks as one of the favourites. This may be due in large part to its familiarity: even people who have little knowledge of quilt designs seem to recognize a log cabin quilt. However, another underlying reason may be that it symbolizes the settlement of a continent, representing home in a hostile environment. Although log cabin quilts were made in Europe, the design is largely associated with the United States and the early settlers, and this enduring quilt pattern has maintained its popularity up until the present day.

Examine the construction of a single log cabin block and you will find it quite straightforward; strips of fabric rotate around a centre square which was traditionally red, to represent the fire or hearth. The block is split diagonally into light and dark fabrics to create the illusion of shadows and flickering firelight within the cabin.

There are many variations in the construction of the log cabin block, but they all rely on this visual play of light and dark tonal values. The blocks can be set together to produce an extraordinary variety of designs, three of the favourites being barn raising, straight furrow and courthouse steps. The size of the basic block can be changed by varying the width of the strips or the size of the centre square.

BASIC LOG CABIN BLOCK –
Shading and Numbered Sequence of Stitching

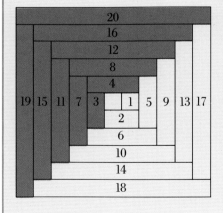

LOG CABIN BLOCK spiral arrangement of strips

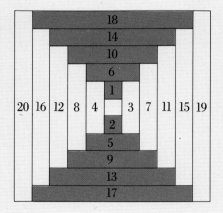

COURT HOUSE STEPS In this variation strips are sewn either side of the centre square

Traditional Log Cabin Quilt

This traditional log cabin quilt is made up of English printed dress cottons and dates from about 1860. The blocks are made in the spiral method, each one having five rounds of strips around the centre square. They are set together with the dark and light sides of each block set opposite each other, which creates strong diagonal lines moving across the quilt surface. The size of the quilt is approximately 80 in (200 cm) by 96 in (242 cm). Thirty 16 in (41 cm) blocks are needed for a quilt this size.

MATERIALS REQUIRED

The log cabin is an ideal design for a scrap quilt, so a good collection of fabrics in pure cotton or polycotton is necessary. If you are buying new fabrics, eleven different ones are needed for the quilt top; five in light and five in dark tones and one for the centre squares in the following amounts, calculated on 45 in (115 cm) wide fabric:

- For the centre square – ½ yd (metre)
  Strips 1 & 2 – ½ yd (metre) light
  Strips 3 & 4 – ½ yd (metre) dark
  Strips 5 & 6 – ¾ yd (metre) light
  Strips 7 & 8 – ¾ yd (metre) dark
  Strips 9 & 10 – 1 yd (metre) light
  Strips 11 & 12 – 1 yd (metre) dark
  Strips 13 & 14 – 1 yd (metre) light
  Strips 15 & 16 – 1¼ yd (metre) dark
  Strips 17 & 18 – 1¼ yd (metre) light
  Strips 19 & 20 – 1½ yd (metre) dark
- The size of the completed quilt top is 96 in × 80 in (242 cm × 200 cm), so a piece of cotton backing 100 in × 84 in (2.60 m × 2.10 m) and a piece of wadding (batting) the same size are required.

METHOD OF CONSTRUCTION

For a 16 in (41 cm) block made up of five rounds of strips, the finished size of the centre square needs to be 3½ in (9 cm) across, and the strips need to be 1¼ in (32 mm) wide, so add ¼ in (6 mm) seam allowance all round when cutting out. Cut fabric for the centre square 4 in × 4 in (10 cm × 10 cm) and the strips 1¾ in (4.5 cm) wide. This block can be made by hand or machine; a running stitch ¼ in (6 mm) from the cut edge is used to stitch fabrics together (see Chapter 2).

PREPARATION

Sort fabrics into light and dark values; plain or patterned fabrics can be used, or a combination of the two. The important point is to have two contrasting groups of fabrics.

Cut the strips on the straight grain of the fabric either lengthwise or crosswise. Mark the strips by drawing directly onto the fabric with a fabric marker. If you are using new fabric a rotary cutter and board will speed up cutting (see Chapter 1). Cut

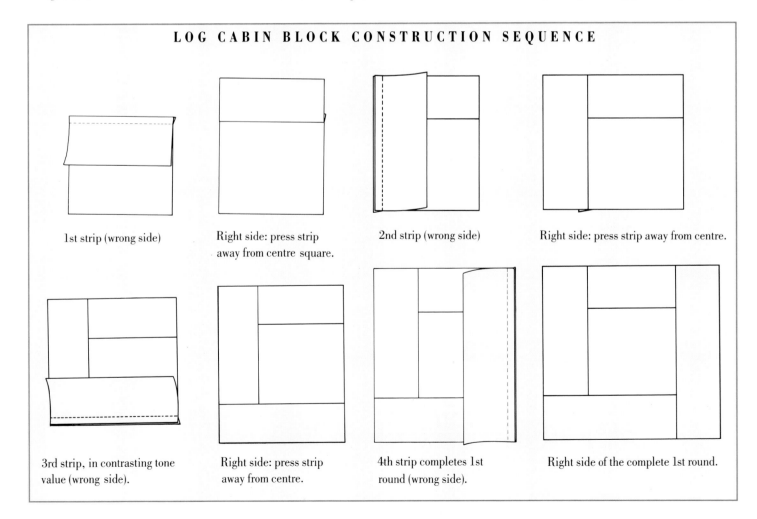

LOG CABIN BLOCK CONSTRUCTION SEQUENCE

1st strip (wrong side)

Right side: press strip away from centre square.

2nd strip (wrong side)

Right side: press strip away from centre.

3rd strip, in contrasting tone value (wrong side).

Right side: press strip away from centre.

4th strip completes 1st round (wrong side).

Right side of the complete 1st round.

ABOVE Straight Furrow.

~

the strips accurately, as any inaccuracy in cutting out will transfer itself to the stitching, and then to the finished blocks, it will create blocks of unequal sizes, and cause difficulty in fitting them together, resulting ultimately in unevenness in the appearance of the overall quilt design.

There are no points to match in the log cabin block, and if accuracy is carefully maintained in the cutting and stitching this is an easy one to construct.

MAKING UP THE BLOCKS

Cut the centre squares; they should measure 4 in by 4 in (10 cm by 10 cm). Then select the fabric to be used for the first strip. Cut a length to fit the side of the square and pin right sides together. Stitch ¼ in (6 mm) from the edge. On the wrong side press the seam towards the strip. Using the same fabric for strip 2,

cut another length to fit the edge of the square plus the added width of strip 1. Pin, stitch and press as before.

The third and fourth strips are cut from the contrasting tone-value group. Cut strip 3 the length of the square plus the edge of strip 2; pin, stitch and press. The fourth strip completes the first round.

Continue adding strips, increasing the length of each to accommodate the width of the previous strip, and placing light and dark fabrics in the correct sequence. The strips can rotate in a clockwise or anti-clockwise direction, but must be consistent in all blocks and not change direction.

When you have made 30 blocks lay them together using the picture as a guide and stitch, taking in ¼ in (6 mm) seam allowance. Stitch the blocks together in groups of four or six first, rather than in long

lines. If they are slightly different sizes, the longer the seams the more difficult it becomes to match points between the blocks. By stitching together in groups of four or six, any slight inaccuracies in size can be eased to fit. Press open the seams between the blocks as matching points is easier with open seams.

The patchwork top is now complete. In the antique quilt illustrated there is no border; the block setting extends to the edge of the quilt. Alternatively, a narrow binding would be an appropriate way to finish this quilt.

Assemble the quilt top, wadding (batting) and backing as described in the section on basic methods (Chapter 2) and quilt by hand or machine.

LEFT *Diamond Log*
Cabin quilt.
~

The Diamond Log Cabin Quilt

The Blazing Star design was one favoured by the expert needlewoman to show off her skills in a masterpiece quilt, and the graphic qualities of this design are added to those of the Log Cabin by altering the shape of the block centres in this quilt. The blocks are constructed in the same way as the square log cabin, with strips rotating around a central piece, but the central piece is a diamond rather than a square. The same principles of light and shade manipulation are used to dynamic effect. When the blocks are set together in a large six-pointed star, with the dark sides of the block innermost, a pattern of radiating hexagons emerges. The red diamond centres of each of the fifty-four blocks pivot the eye around the star shape. The possible problem of fitting this shape into a final frame has been solved by making the quilt a large hexagon, filling the negative space with six plain diamonds which reflect each segment of the centre star. A striped border of darker fabrics edges the quilt. The centre-star shape is tied rather than quilted so there is no surface stitch-ing to detract from the central pattern, whilst the outer diamonds are closely quilted by machine. The size of the quilt is approximately 100 in (260 cm) wide.

MATERIALS REQUIRED
Based on 45 in (115 cm) wide fabric –
◼ For the centre diamonds – ½ yd (metre)
   Strips 1 & 2 – ½ yd (metre) light
   Strips 3 & 4 – ½ yd (metre) dark
   Strips 5 & 6 – ½ yd (metre) light
   Strips 7 & 8 – ½ yd (metre) dark
   Strips 9 & 10 – ½ yd (metre) light
   Strips 11 & 12 – ½ yd (metre) dark

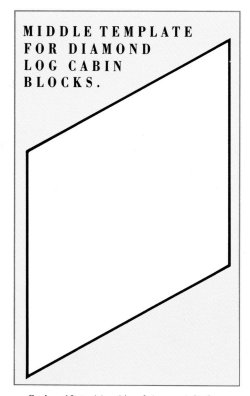

MIDDLE TEMPLATE
FOR DIAMOND
LOG CABIN
BLOCKS.

Strips 13 & 14 – ½ yd (metre) light
Strips 15 & 16 – ½ yd (metre) dark
▌For the border – ¾ yd (metre) of each
fabric to be used.
▌For the large plain diamonds – 2½ yd
(metre) of 60 in (150 cm) wide fabric.
▌Wadding (batting) 100 in (2.60 m)
square.

MAKING UP THE BLOCKS
Trace the centre template and cut out the
diamond centres in your chosen fabric.
The finished width of the strips is ½ in
(13 mm) so cut them 1 in (25 mm) wide to
allow a ¼ in (6 mm) seam allowance each
side. The first two strips are light coloured.
Lay a strip along one side of the diamond
centre with the right sides together, leaving enough fabric each end to trim to the
correct angle after stitching. Stitch, taking in a ¼ in (6 mm) seam allowance. On
the wrong side press the seam towards
the diamond centre and trim the ends of
the strip in line with the sides of the diamond, maintaining the correct angle.
Add strip 2 in the same light fabric, stitch,
press and trim as before.

Strips 3 and 4 are dark coloured. Add
the third strip stitching, pressing and
trimming as before.

*ABOVE A Blazing Star
quilt, machine pieced and
hand quilted, made of
cotton and other fabrics.
~
BELOW Front and back
views of a single
Diamond Log Cabin
block.
~*

Strip 4 completes the first round of strips. Continue to add strips keeping the light and dark fabrics in sequence until four rounds have been completed. Fifty-four log cabin blocks are required for the six-pointed star.

JOINING THE BLOCKS

Begin by making the six sections of the star from nine blocks each. In order to join diamond shapes together, the seam allowance, rather than the cut edge, needs to be aligned, so that when the diamonds are opened out flat after stitching you have a straight edge (see piecing angled shapes, Chapter 2).

Join rows of three blocks and press seams open at this stage. Then, matching seams, join the rows of three to produce a large diamond made up of nine blocks. Remember to keep the darker sides of the blocks all pointing one way.

Before joining the star points together, make a template from one of them for the plain diamonds. Join the sections in two sets of three, darker sides of the blocks innermost, then put the two halves together and stitch the final seam across the centre of the star. Leave a ¼ in (6 mm) unstitched at each inner angle of the star. Press these seams open.

Carefully position the six plain diamonds between the star points, then pin and stitch. At the inner angle of the points, turn the plain diamonds through the unstitched seam allowance. Press the plain diamond seam towards the star.

THE BORDER STRIPS

Using the darker fabrics cut a series of strips 1½ in (4 cm) wide and the length of each of the six sides. By having fewer or more strips, or altering the widths, the size of the quilt can be adjusted. Work around the edge of the quilt, trimming the ends of the strips to fit the angle of the hexagon. Save the final, outer strip as a binding to enclose wadding and backing. Make sure you cut the backing when the final strip is on, to achieve the right size for it. Assemble the quilt, tack (baste), tie the coloured part and quilt the outer, white parts by hand or machine.

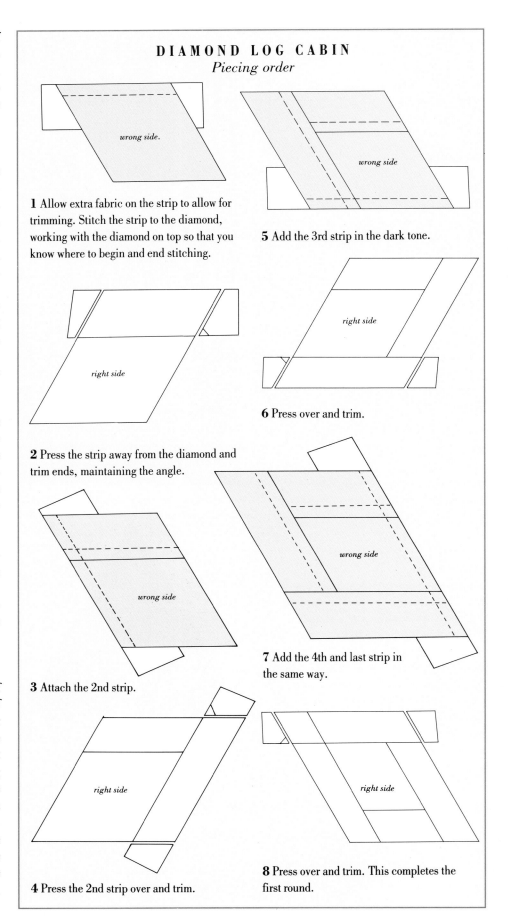

DIAMOND LOG CABIN
Piecing order

1 Allow extra fabric on the strip to allow for trimming. Stitch the strip to the diamond, working with the diamond on top so that you know where to begin and end stitching.

2 Press the strip away from the diamond and trim ends, maintaining the angle.

3 Attach the 2nd strip.

4 Press the 2nd strip over and trim.

5 Add the 3rd strip in the dark tone.

6 Press over and trim.

7 Add the 4th and last strip in the same way.

8 Press over and trim. This completes the first round.

JOINING THE DIAMOND BLOCKS TOGETHER

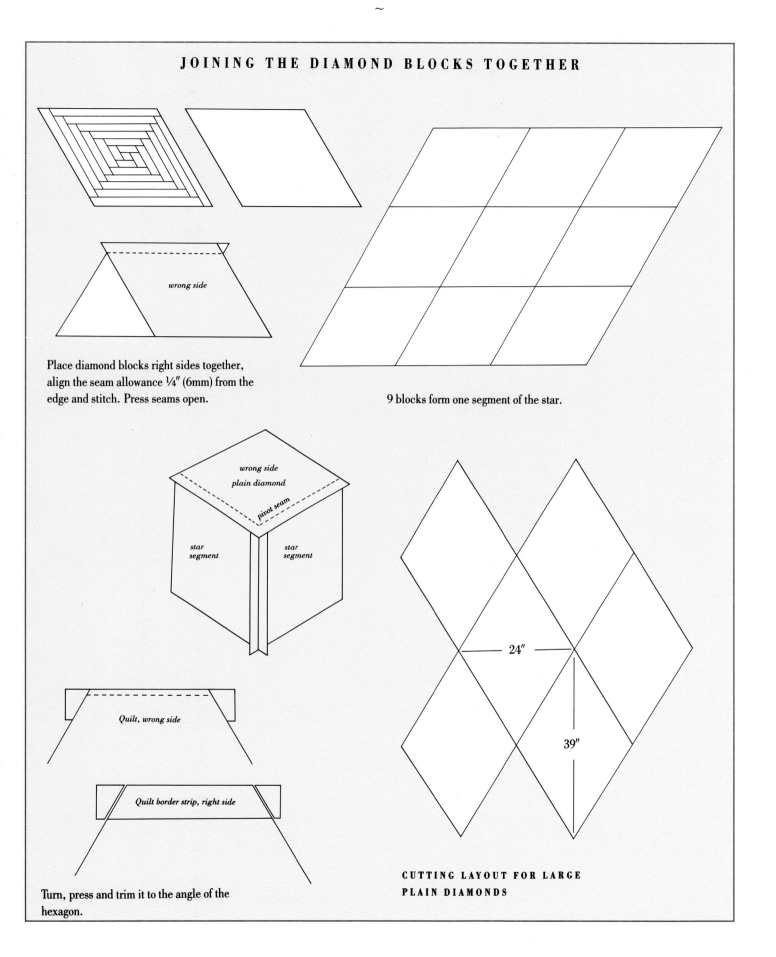

Place diamond blocks right sides together, align the seam allowance ¼″ (6mm) from the edge and stitch. Press seams open.

9 blocks form one segment of the star.

wrong side

wrong side
plain diamond
pivot seam

star segment   *star segment*

Quilt, wrong side

Quilt border strip, right side

Turn, press and trim it to the angle of the hexagon.

24″

39″

CUTTING LAYOUT FOR LARGE PLAIN DIAMONDS

Log Cabin Windows

This quilt is a contemporary interpretation of the traditional log cabin block, set in the 'light and dark' or 'sunshine and shadow' variation. Each set of four blocks has the lighter sides set together making strong, light diamonds. The red fabrics used on the dark sides of the centre blocks are carried half-way into the edging and corner blocks, giving a diffused appear-

ABOVE Log Cabin Windows.

~

ance to the centre of the quilt. The viewer has to look closely into the quilt's surface at first to identify the secondary, darker diamonds, but once established the dark and light diamonds seem to shift, increasing the impression of a garden glimpsed through tiny windows. This is created by

the block centres, which are not a plain square, but a tiny nine-patch of floral fabric embroidered with satin stitch in a multi-coloured thread.

The 'logs' or strips of each block are folded and applied to a base fabric giving the quilt added surface texture. This is a development of the technique used in some old log cabin quilts where the pieced fabric was stitched onto squares of backing, thereby dispensing with the need for a filler. Once the quilt top is completed all that is needed is a backing sheet to conceal the seams. This folding and stitching makes a rather heavy quilt which is therefore more suitable for a wall hanging or throw than for use as a bedspread.

MATERIALS REQUIRED

The same principles apply as for other log cabin quilts. This is a scrap quilt so a good selection of light and dark fabrics is needed, and because they are to be folded, cotton lawn is ideal; its light weight and close weave make it easy to handle and fine enough to take the folding without becoming too heavy.

▮ You also need 2½ yd (metre) of bondaweb which is ½ yd (metre) wide. Bondaweb is a fabric glue bonded onto a paper backing. It is placed against the wrong side of the fabric with the glue side, which feels slightly rougher than the paper side, face down, and ironed on. The paper can then be peeled away leaving a patch of fabric glue to which other fabrics can be bonded with a medium iron. (Its use for this quilt will be explained later.)

▮ For the base squares: 3¼ yd (metre) of white cotton sheeting 60 in (150 cm) wide.

▮ Backing material: a piece of cotton 64 in (155 cm) square.

▮ Machine embroidery thread: Madeira multi-coloured shade 2103, 500 metre reel was used on this quilt, although any other plain or shaded thread can be used.

▮ Sewing-machine with a swing needle.

There are 64 blocks in the quilt made up in sets of four; ie, each set of blocks is made up in the same sequence of fabric for the strips, although the centres are different.

THE BLOCK CENTRES

Cut the sheeting into 10 in (26 cm) squares and find the centre point of each by ironing diagonal lines across. Draw a 5 in (13 cm) square in the centre. Cut a 5 in (13 cm) square of bondaweb and iron this onto the marked out square, then peel off the paper backing. Cut out the nine patches to the exact size of the templates given in the diagram. Lay the patches onto the 5 in (13 cm) square of bondaweb, overlapping

ABOVE Detail showing folded strips.
~

them very slightly (about 3 mm). This will prevent the raw edges lifting under the satin stitch. Now iron down the patches to stick them to the backing.

Satin stitch over the raw edges (you will find it easier to get a straight line if you do a row of straight stitching first) using the decorative thread. Now mark the 'frame' (see diagram) and stitch it in satin stitch also.

THE STRIPS

The strips are arranged in the spiral way. Although only ½ in (13 mm) of fabric is revealed on each strip, another ¾ in (19 mm) must lie under the next row of strips because the stitching is ½ in (13 mm) from the folded edges and must catch in the raw edges of the preceding row. The first two rounds of strips are therefore cut 2½ in (6.5 cm) wide, then folded in half lengthwise and pressed to give the correct final width of the strip.

FIRST ROUND

Remember that the blocks are worked four at a time. Select fabric for strips 1 and 2 from the light values. Strip 1 is 5 in (13 cm) long and strip 2 is 5½ in (14 cm) long, so for four blocks, cut a strip totalling 42 in long by 2½ in wide (107 cm by 6.5 cm). Fold the fabric in half lengthwise and press, then mark the stitching line ½ in (13 mm) from the folded edge. Divide it into four lengths of 5 in (13 cm) for the first side, and four more 5½ in (14 cm) long for the second side. Take a 5 in

(13 cm) strip and place the folded edge against the 'window-frame' on the block centre. Pin and stitch along the line marked ½ in (13 mm) from the folded edge. Use matching thread. Repeat on the other three blocks.

Now give the block a quarter turn and place a 5½ in (14 cm) strip against the frame stitching on the second side and across the end of the first strip. Stitch ½ in (13 mm) from the folded edge along the marked line. Repeat on the other three blocks.

Strips 3 and 4 are in dark values. Select the fabric and for four blocks cut a length of 46 in long by 2½ in wide (117 cm by 6.5 cm). Press in half as before, mark a stitching line ½ in (13 mm) from the folded edge and divide into four pieces 5½ in (14 cm) long, and four 6 in (15.5 cm) long. Place a 5½ in (14 cm) strip against the frame stitching on the third side of the window and stitch as before using matching thread. Position a 6 in (15.5 cm) strip on the fourth side and stitch along the marked line. Repeat on the other three blocks.

The first round is now complete. The corner and side patches of the central square will have been reduced to the same size as the centre patch, and the stitching will have caught the raw edges of the patches, leaving a ½ in (13 mm) fold free.

Templates and layout for miniature nine-patch block centres for 'LOG CABIN WINDOWS' quilt.

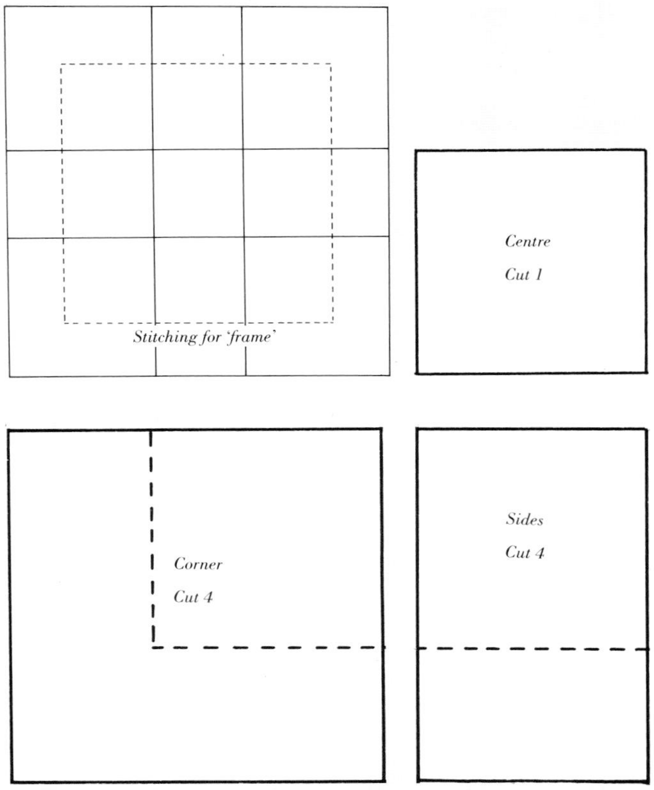

Centre
Cut 1

Stitching for 'frame'

Corner
Cut 4

Sides
Cut 4

SECOND ROUND

Prepare the fabric for the second round as for the first round. Strips 5 and 6 are in a light fabric and are 6 in (15.5 cm) and 6½ in (16.5 cm) long. Strips 7 and 8 are in a dark fabric and are 6½ in (16.5 cm) and 7 in (18 cm) long. Cut, fold and press them, and mark the stitching line. Position them against the stitching on the first round, and attach along the stitching line, rotating the block as before.

THIRD ROUND

We must now look ahead to the fourth round of strips. The fourth round lies flat against the backing, instead of being folded, in order to reduce bulk when joining the blocks together. This affects the third round of strips as the extra ¾ in (1.9 cm) beyond the stitching lines as on rounds 1 and 2 is not necessary, strip 4 requiring only ¼ in (6 mm) seam allowance.

The third round of strips should be cut 1½ in (4 cm) wide, which when folded in half will give ¾ in (19 mm) wide strips. All the strips in round three are 7¼ in (18.5 cm) long, so for the four blocks cut a length 58 in long by 1½ in wide (148 cm by 4 cm) from light fabric and 58 in long by 1½ in wide (148 cm by 4 cm) from dark fabric. Fold the strips in half, press and mark the stitching line ½ in (13 mm) from the fold and divide each length into

CHART OF MEASUREMENTS FOR FOLDED STRIPS						
	STRIP NO.	WIDTH		LENGTH		TONE VALUE
ROUND 1	1	2½in	6.5cm	5in	13cm	light
	2	2½in	6.5cm	5½in	14cm	light
	3	2½in	6.5cm	5½in	14cm	dark
	4	2½in	6.5cm	6in	15.5cm	dark
ROUND 2	5	2½in	6.5cm	6in	15.5cm	light
	6	2½in	6.5cm	6½in	16.5cm	light
	7	2½in	6.5cm	6½in	16.5cm	dark
	8	2½in	6.5cm	7in	18cm	dark
ROUND 3	9	1½in	4cm	7¼in	18.5cm	light
	10	1½in	4cm	7¼in	18.5cm	light
	11	1½in	4cm	7¼in	18.5cm	dark
	12	1½in	4cm	7¼in	18.5cm	dark
ROUND 4	13	1¼in	3.5cm	7½in	19cm	light
	14	1¼in	3.5cm	8in	20.5cm	light
	15	1¼in	3.5cm	8½in	21.5cm	dark
	16	1¼in	3.5cm	9in	23cm	dark

ABOVE RIGHT

Log Cabin Windows
Block. Stage 3, three
rounds of strips in
position.

~

RIGHT

Log Cabin Windows –
one completed block.

~

eight equal strips. Place the fold of each strip against the previous line of stitching on round 2 and stitch down strips 9, 10, 11 and 12 on all four blocks, rotating in the correct sequence.

FOURTH ROUND

Measure and cut the fourth round as follows:

▌In light values –
Strip 13 – 1½ in × 7½ in (4 cm × 19 cm)
Strip 14 – 1½ in × 8 in (4 cm × 20.5 cm)
▌In dark values –
Strip 15 – 1½ in × 8½ in (4 cm × 22 cm)
  Strip 16 – 1½ in × 9 in (4 cm × 23 cm).

Place strip 13 right side down against strip 9 so you have three raw edges together. Tack (baste) and turn the block over. Now stitch just inside the previous row of stitching on the back of the block, to ensure that the stitching on round 3 does not show on the front of the block. Turn back over, remove the tacking and fold the strip over to reveal the right side of the fabric; press this flat against the backing.

Repeat this process with strips 14, 15 and 16, rotating the block and pressing each strip flat as you work. Repeat on the other three blocks.

The fourth round is now complete. Measure ¾ in (19 mm) from the last seam and draw a line around the outside of the block on the front. Stitch along this line with a straight stitch to fasten the final round of strips to the backing, and trim away excess fabric close to this line of stitching. This gives a ¼ in (6 mm) seam allowance round each block for joining the blocks together.

JOINING THE BLOCKS
Refer to the picture and arrange the blocks in order. Join them in sets of four, and

ABOVE Roofs and Windows quilt.
~

RIGHT A detail of Roofs and Windows showing the border and decorative stitching.
~

OPPOSITE, TOP In this small quilt (Log Cabin Windows) the darker sides of the same blocks have been put together to form strong dark crosses.
~

join these in sets of four again. Join these up to make the two halves of the quilt.

Finally, stitch one long seam across the middle. Press all the seams open as you go. Turn ¼ in (6 mm) in all around the outside of the quilt, tack it down and press.

BACKING THE QUILT AND FINISHING

This type of log cabin quilt does not need any wadding (batting) as the base squares form the filler. Smooth the 64 in (155 cm) square cotton backing over the back of the quilt, then pin and tack the layers together. Trim the backing to ½ in (13 mm) around the edge and turn this raw edge inside so that the edges of the quilt top and backing are even. Tack (baste) the two layers together round the edge and remove the previous tacking. Stitch the quilt top to the backing by sewing machine, stitching in the 'ditch' of the seams between the blocks. Start with the centre seams and work outwards. Use either a neutral-coloured thread that will blend in with all the colours, or an invisible filament, with thread to match the backing in the bobbin.

Finally, slip hem the quilt top to the back by hand all around the outside edge of the quilt.

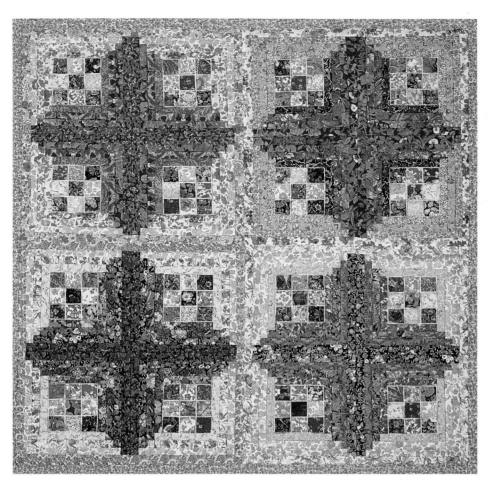

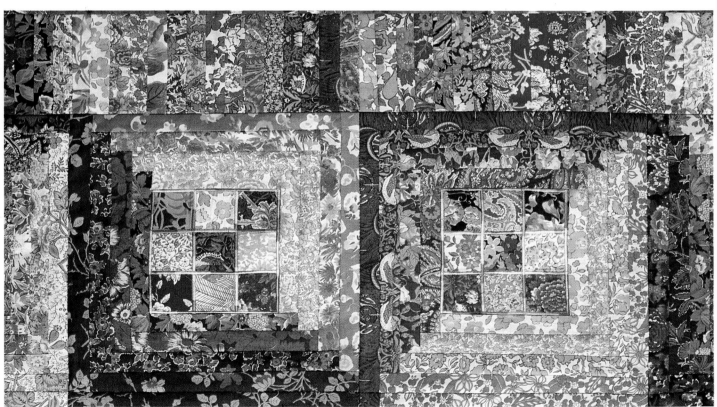

Chapter Six

CATHEDRAL WINDOW

~

Blue Illusion

~

"*B*arbara Brackman, MA, a noted Kansas quilt historian, gave a paper to the American Quilt Study Group in 1980. In it she says that in 1933 a pamphlet The Quilt Fair Comes to You, was published, in which "patterns from quilts shown at the Chicago World's Fair", and others, were advertised. This booklet seems to be the first publication of the pattern we now call Cathedral Window. Here it was called the "Daisy Quilt". "

Sheila Betterton, *Quilters Guild Newsletter*. Spring, 1983.

Cathedral Window patchwork is made by joining folding foundation squares of fabric. These small panels are decorated with other fabrics. Because of the folding and stitching, no quilting is needed as the end result is several layers thick, and these layers are stitched through when the panels of decorative fabric are applied.

Blue Illusion

By using striped fabric for the background, and rich little fragments of exotic silk, satin and velvet, the maker of this quilt has exploited the full potential of the technique. Folding and stitching has turned the black, purple and turquoise stripes in all directions, and the placing of the inserted pieces, concentrating the reds in the top corner, gives the impression of a glowing light through stained glass. Some of the panels are left unfilled, revealing the stripes, while others at the edge of the quilt sometimes stray into the border of narrow strips. These strips have been skilfully graduated through the tones, colours and textures of the fabrics round the quilt's edge. The quilt is finished with a bias binding.

CATHEDRAL WINDOW
Preparing the squares by hand

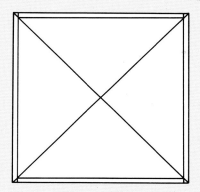

Turn a narrow hem and press. Find the centre point of the square by folding and pressing.

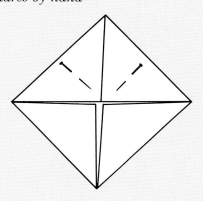

Turn the corners to the centre point and pin down. Press again to crease the outer fold.

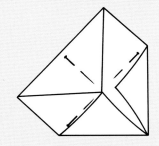

Fold the corners to the centre again.

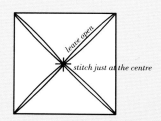

Stitch across the centre to fasten the corners.

CATHEDRAL WINDOWS
Preparing the squares by machine

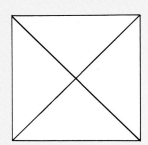

Fold the square in half and stitch up the sides taking ¼″ (6mm) seam allowance.

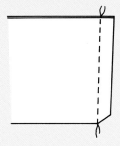

Clip the corners off the seams on the folded side and press the seams open.

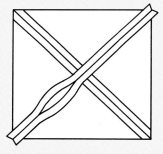

At the open side, place the seams together and stitch, leaving a gap to turn the square through to the right side.

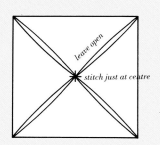

Turn to the right side through the gap, poke corners out and press.

Fold the corners to the centre and stitch down, at the centre only.

CATHEDRAL WINDOWS
Joining the squares

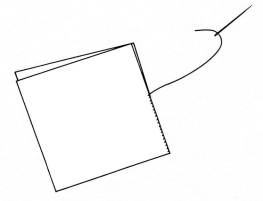

When you have prepared enough squares, place them right sides together and join along one edge with whip stitch from corner to corner.

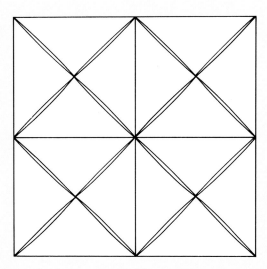

Join as many squares as you need for your design

CATHEDRAL WINDOW
Stitching in the decorative fabric

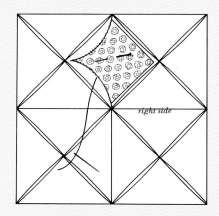

right side   *4 squares joined*

Measure the space between two of the background squares and cut pieces of decorative fabric in that size. Turn the folded edge of the background over the decorative squares and hem down neatly all round.

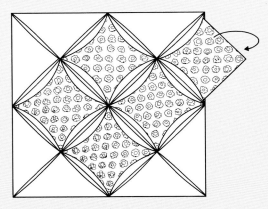

At the edges, hem the backing over two sides of the decorative square. Fold the remaining half of the decorative square to the back. Neaten the edges and hem down.

*RIGHT Detail of Blue
Illusion.
~*

Chapter Seven

AN APPROACH
TO ORIGINAL
DESIGN

~

Door Curtain 2.

~

" The Art Quilt has emerged, and it heralds a dramatic and fundamental change in the history of quilts. "

Penny McMorris & Michael Kile, *The Art Quilt*, 1986.

Door Curtain 1

This quilt was made to hang as a curtain in front of a large door, and the influences on its design are architectural, referring to the intended purpose of the quilt. The central panel is made of horizontal strips of red triangles, and is flanked by columns of rectangles in turquoise and purple. Small red silk triangles have been inserted between the seams of the rectangles, giving three dimensional detail to the quilt.

Across the top of the quilt rays of a red fan-light design radiate upwards, reinforcing the architectural theme. The fabrics used are cotton, taffeta and silk. Quilting is by machine. The size of the quilt is 100 in × 48 in (254 cm × 122 cm).

Door Curtain 2

This second door curtain also has references to architectural detail. Although the pattern shapes of the two panels are identical, different fabrics have been used for each one to provide variety to the centre, which has strong diagonal lines.

Narrow, dark blue bands separate these two panels from the side and centre columns of narrow strips. These strips also carry the three-dimensional triangles inserted between the seams, this time in double rows. The quilt is finished at the top and bottom with bands of geometric shapes. Machine-quilting in straight and satin stitch adds a final decorative detail.

Single Block Design

These single blocks illustrate the technique used in making the patterns for the door curtains. Try this approach to original design by starting with a single block before progressing to larger and more ambitious projects.

THE DESIGN

Start by drawing between six and eight 2-in (5-cm) squares on a sheet of paper. Then, using ruler and pencil, divide each square into between 10–15 shapes.

OPPOSITE PAGE *Possible designs for single block 'original design'.*

RIGHT *Door curtain 1.*

~   ~

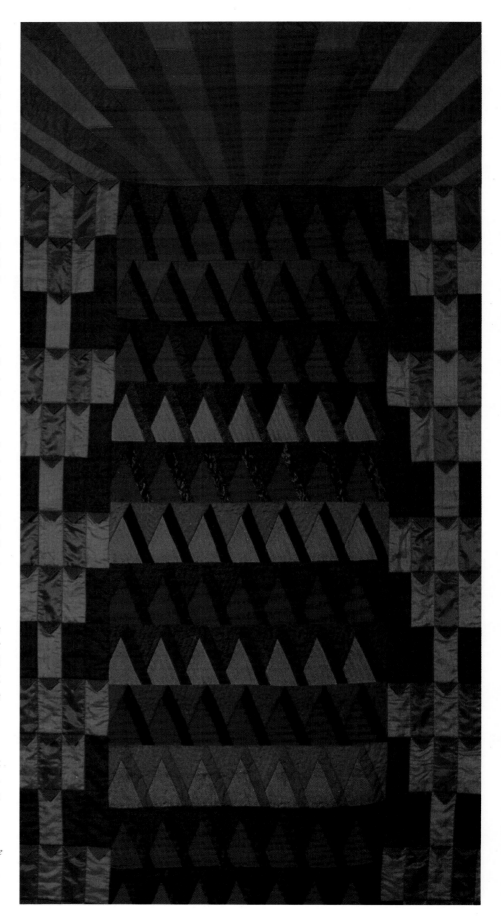

At this preliminary stage do not think too hard about creating a 'good design'. The important point is to get some designs down on paper from which you can select a suitable one. Try to vary the shapes and sizes for visual interest and avoid any shapes with a very narrow angle (less than 30°) as this may present problems in joining the pieces together.

The next step is to select a design that appeals to you from the ones you have drawn and draw it up to the actual size the block is to be. From 12 in to 16 in (30 cm to 40 cm) is a good size to start with. Number the pieces on your drawing in order of construction. Remember the rules established for the traditional blocks: it is easiest to start with the smaller shapes and work towards the larger ones.

Now make a full size tracing of your block design complete with numbers. This is your construction key.

MAKING THE PATTERN

Cut up your full size drawing accurately and stick each piece face up on to thin card. Then, using a quilter's quarter, add ¼ in (6 mm) seam allowance *all round* each piece and cut out. Mark the fabric grain on the pattern pieces by referring to the tracing.

CUTTING OUT

Place the numbered pattern pieces face down on the wrong side of the fabric, mark round the outside edges and cut out the shapes.

Assemble the pieces jig-saw style on a flat surface using the tracing as a guide. Stitch the block together using ¼ in (6 mm) allowances and pressing seams as you go – open if stitching on a sewing machine, to the darker side if sewing by hand (see Chapter 2).

Different effects can be achieved with the same block pattern by varying the fabrics used, or repeating the blocks in regular or random combinations.

These patterns can be used to make single block items, for example cushion covers (pillows), or they can be used in multiples to make larger panels for wall hangings or quilts.

Assemble with the wadding (batting) and backing and quilt by hand or machine. On the examples illustrated the quilting is done with a straight and satin stitch on the sewing-machine.

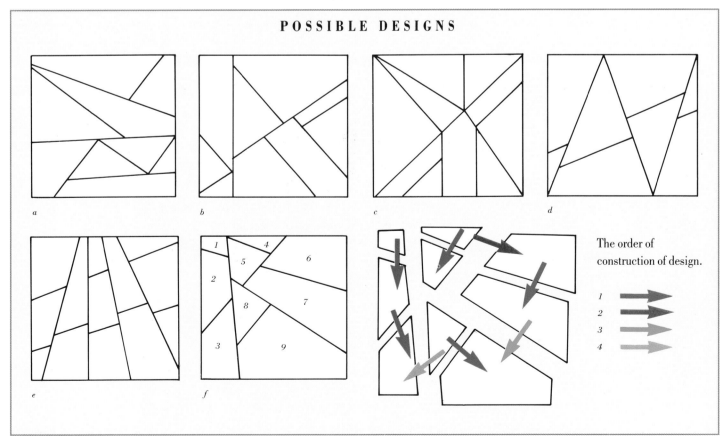

POSSIBLE DESIGNS

a

b

c

d

e

f

The order of construction of design.

1

2

3

4

GLOSSARY

~

APPLIQUÉ The decorative technique of cutting out pieces of material and stitching them to a foundation.

BASTE See *tack*.

BATTING See *wadding*.

BIAS GRAIN The diagonal of the fabric. To find the true bias, cut a square of fabric the size of the width and fold diagonally from corner to corner.

COMFORTER A heavy bed-cover filled with insulating material, duckdown or wadding (batting), and quilted to keep it in place.

BLOCK The design unit on which American patchwork is based. Usually geometric shapes which will fit into a grid, and which are repeated across the surface of the quilt are used.

Blocks are usually square but can be rectangular, and can be made in other shapes as well.

DOMETTE A form of interlining which gives weight and warmth to curtains and wall-hung quilts made of woven cotton or polyester.

PIECING The sewing together of small pieces of fabric to form a larger whole piece.

QUILT A fabric sandwich made up of three layers: the top is often decorative patchwork; the filler gives warmth; the backing forms the lining.

QUILTING The stitches which secure the three layers of a quilt – top, filler and backing – together. Traditionally done in a small hand-sewn running stitch.

STRAIGHT GRAIN The way the threads lie in a piece of fabric. The weft threads are woven between the warp threads.

SET The way a block is used in a quilt (see Chapter 4, American Patchwork).

TACK (BASTE) Temporary stitches to hold fabric in place until smaller, more secure stitching is done. In English patchwork, tacking (basting) is also used to hold papers in fabric until shapes are stitched together. Large running stitches that can be removed easily should be used.

TEMPLATE The pattern from which patchwork shapes are cut. They are made of stiff material such as card, plastic or metal.

TIED QUILT A quilt in which the three layers are secured together at regular intervals with knots.

WADDING (BATTING) The insulating filler in a quilt.

WALKING FOOT An attachment available for some sewing-machines. It feeds more than one layer of fabric evenly through the machine, preventing the top layer from being pushed along faster than the other layers.

FURTHER READING

~

Beyer, Jinny, *The Scrap Look*, (EPM Publications: 1985).

Betterton, Shiela, *Quilts & Coverlets from the American Museum*, 1978, and *More Quilts & Coverlets from the American Museum* 1988, The American Museum in Britain, Bath England.

Cooper, Patricia, & Bradley Buferd, Norma, *The Quilters, Women and Domestic Art, An Oral History*, (Anchor Press/Doubleday: 1978).

Finley, Ruth, E., *Old Patchwork Quilts and the Women who made Them*, (Charles T. Branford: 1929).

Gutcheon, Beth, *The Perfect Patchwork Primer*, (Penguin: 1973).

James, Michael, *The Quiltmaker's Handbook*, (Prentice-Hall: 1978).

James, Michael, *The Second Quiltmaker's Handbook*, (Prentice-Hall: 1981).

McMorris, Penny & Kile, Michael, *The Art Quilt*, (The Quilt Digest Press: 1986).

Walker, Michele, *Quiltmaking in Patchwork and Appliqué*, (Ebury Press: 1985).

INDEX

~